WRITING DEVELOPMENT

Open University Press

English, Language, and Education series

General Editor: Anthony Adams

Lecturer in Education, University of Cambridge

TITLES IN THE SERIES

WRITING DEVELOPMENT
Magic in the brain

Roslyn Arnold

Open University Press
Milton Keynes · Philadelphia

To Louisa

Open University Press
Celtic Court
22 Ballmoor
Buckingham
MK18 1XW

and
1900 Frost Road, Suite 101
Bristol, PA 19007, USA

First published 1991

British Library Cataloguing in Publication Data
Arnold, Roslyn *1945–*
   Writing development: magic in the brain.—(English,
   language and education series).
   1. Children. Written communication
   I. Title   II. Series
   372.623

   ISBN 0-335-15195-7

Library of Congress Cataloging-in-Publication Data

Arnold, Roslyn 1945–
      Writing development : magic in the brain / Roslyn Arnold.
         p.   cm.—(English, language, and education series)
      Includes bibliographical references and index.
      ISBN 0-335-15195-7
      1. Children—Writing.   2. Writing—Evaluation.   3. Children as
   authors—Case studies.   I. Title.   II. Series.
   LB1139.W7A74   1991
   372.6′23—dc20   90-27371
                                                CIP

Typeset by Rowland Phototypesetting Limited
Bury St Edmunds, Suffolk
Printed in Great Britain by St Edmundsbury Press Limited
Bury St Edmunds, Suffolk

Contents

Acknowledgements

This book owes much to the students I worked with as a writing teacher/researcher for four years on the study which inspired it. Although their names have been changed here, I hope their identities and voices are very much in evidence. I would like to thank Emeritus Professor Don Spearritt for his scholarly supervision of my research and Professor Andrew Wilkinson, Bruce Bennett and Patrick (CTP) Diamond for their insightful comments on the thesis. My heartfelt thanks also to Janice Folletta, Ken Watson and Wayne Sawyer for help and advice during the four-year study; Anthony Adams and Ken Watson for comments on drafts of this book; Michael Griffiths and David Hardy for their scientific reactions to the spiral model; Professors Mary K. Croft and Helen Heaton for the opportunity to present my views at the Rites of Writing/WCTE conferences at the University of Wisconsin, Stevens Point, USA; my sister Cynthia Gregory-Roberts for support, advice and forbearance; Joan Wood for very practical help and my daughter Louisa for some quotations, and patience beyond her years.

General editor's introduction

It is a great pleasure to introduce the first full-length book by Roslyn Arnold to be published in this country. She may already be known to readers of this series as a contributing author to several of the books we have published and I have long been an admirer of her work in the University of Sydney.

At the present emerging stage of the National Curriculum in England and Wales we need as much help and advice as we can obtain from sources outside ourselves about the processes through which we are going. Roslyn does, in fact, refer to the Cox Report, the basis for the National Curriculum in English in her own Introduction. She expresses there a concern, shared by many of us, that the proposed levels of attainment may be applied in too simplistic and mechanistic a manner.

The Cox Report does, of course, itself make the point that development in language is recursive rather than linear, but it is tied, through the model on which the National Curriculum has been established, to the need to seek to identify sequential patterns (levels) of development and this may appear, superficially, to be easier in the case of writing than in those of the other language modes. From the point of view of assessment it is easier to 'capture' writing than other modes of expression. It will be the more important, therefore, to develop sensitive measures for the understanding of what is happening in writing and to apply that understanding to its assessment and, more importantly, to the development of young people as writers.

It is such an understanding that is provided by this book. It brings together a good deal of existing psychological theory about writing and confirms our understanding of this through the longitudinal study on which the book's contents are based. Roslyn Arnold's 'spiral model' (fig. 2.1, p. 20) grows out of her own researches and is the starting point for her writing theory. Its usefulness is that it gives us a means of talking about 'growth' and 'development' in rather more precise terms than are often found. It also supplants an overly simple model of linear development and may help teachers in putting flesh on the bones of the National Curriculum.

A major part of the 'flesh' of this book itself is in chapters 4 to 7 with the detailed case studies that these present. As Roslyn Arnold says, we tell stories to illuminate a point of view. I find the stories told here speak to me very clearly of a practised and gifted teacher conducting planned interventions in the classroom so as to develop her young students as writers. (It may be that some teachers will prefer to start with these chapters and return to the theories on which they are based later.) We need more practitioners' theories of writing; we need more strategies for appropriate interventions in the classroom; above all, in the present climate, we need to find more ways of developing writers rather than just of measuring writing development. The idea of 'writing partnerships' described here has some affinity with that described by Morag Styles and her colleagues (1989) but the processes of self-assessment and reflection on one's own writing are applicable to any classroom. They should certainly provide useful insights for the development of Attainment Tasks, 'Standardized' or not, in relation to the National Curriculum.

This is true also of the 'test topics' described in chapter 3 which provide an admirable model for item development to explore writing outcomes. Those readers familiar with the work of the National Writing Project in England and Wales will notice some similarities here, especially in the first of the test topics (*Space*) which explores in an excellently concrete way the reasons why children think they write, and what it means to be a writer. There are some interesting correspondences here between the views of Australian students and those elicited in the National Writing Project's own researches.

I find the various grids provided in table 3.1 especially helpful and it would be an interesting exercise to seek to superimpose these upon the Attainment Targets for writing as they have recently (May 1990) been defined in Orders in Council. What we have here, in a concrete and easy-to-use form, is a language for talking about writing development which I think teachers will find helpful in trying to 'map' the progress of their own young writers.

What seems clear, in the United Kingdom at least, is that we are all going to need to do more measurement of student progress. There will be a temptation to rely upon easily scored measuring techniques and Roslyn Arnold's evaluative instruments here provide a workable and more sophisticated alternative.

What this book demonstrates is that it is possible through good and committed teaching, based upon a clear intellectual understanding of what we are doing, to make progress in education. We need to learn from the successes, as well as the failings of each other's educational systems; this is why I am pleased to have made it possible, through publication in an international series, for Roslyn to share her insights with a wider-ranging English-speaking world.

Anthony Adams

Introduction

The other day a journalist from a metropolitan evening newspaper rang me to discuss a special feature planned on education matters. 'Could you write a piece for students on how to write an essay?' 'Of course, how long?' 'Five hundred words.' I laughed wryly, 'But I'm writing a book on the subject a hundred times longer than that.' Meekly I agreed to the request and faxed the piece through to her office the same day. In five hundred words I condensed fifteen years of work researching and teaching the development of writing abilities. Well, more or less. Then I sat and thought about my book, the realities of writing, the tasks we set our students and how theory and practice relate. What I have in mind here about a psychodynamic and interactive approach to writing development has much to do with writers' psychological processes and their interactions with their readers, with each other, with their books and with their social and cultural environment. That phone call brought me down to earth. I was forced to adapt my ideals to the realities of newspaper journalism – working within its constraints. Many student writers are required to work within similar constraints much of the time. And long before they have found their own writing voice. In my allotted span of five hundred words I tried to encourage my readers to discover a pleasure in writing, to explore their own thoughts and feelings and to read other writers' essays to gain a sense of essay-writing styles and voices. What I was really trying to do was relate the theory of writing development I believe in with the external reality that students' success as writers is often judged by their achievements in examination essay writing. With considerably more scope than journalism allows, I outline here what I have called a psychodynamic theory of writing development. I reflect on the practices and practitioners influencing that theory and suggest, sometimes implicitly, other times explicitly, how such a theory works in practice. In a sense this is a story of one teacher's development of a point of view about writing development; a point of view influenced by her own experiences, and her reading, writing and fortuitous encounters with like-minded practitioners. Most of all, this is a theory influenced by the insights students can give us into their own minds as composers of writing when they feel safe, valued and creative. It was from working as a teacher-researcher with two groups of students over a four-year period (school Years 6–9 inclusive, ages 11–14) to test an hypothesis that certain writing intervention tasks would significantly develop students' writing, that I become increasingly impressed with the complex psychological, cognitive and linguistic processes involved in writing development. This book is, in part, a result of observations I made and insights I gained while working closely with thirty-five experimental students in that four-year period.

When Simon, one of my writing students, wrote to his writing partner, 'These classes probably help me to write better but most of the magic's in the brain', he encapsulated for me the essence of the theory I was working towards and gave me the subtitle of this book. The best discoveries always have some historical precursors and later I'll trace the influences on what I have called 'a psycho-dynamic theory of writing development'.

I have used that term to draw attention to what I regard as the essentially self-centred, self-developing and self-symbolizing process of composing in writing. In that process the mind and heart of the writer are actively engaged in construing a view of the world and experiences. I elaborate on that definition throughout this book. In the past twenty years there have been significant advances in our understanding of how children develop the ability to write to convey meaning. One of the outcomes of these advances is that no longer can we regard writing development as a simple outcome of providing children with pen and paper and instructions to complete a composition in thirty minutes. Issues like the purposes for writing, the audiences to whom the writing is addressed, the processes involved in achieving effective meanings in writing and writers' self-concepts are now, deservedly, receiving attention in many schools and universities.

Although I have concerns about some aspects of the Cox Report (1989) on English for ages 5 to 16 in England and Wales, it is interesting to note the 'main features of current best practice' (3.4) identified in the report. In many respects the aims and practices of 'growth model' teachers are endorsed and mandated. My concerns, however, are with the implementation and testing of the attainment targets stipulated in the report, particularly for their potential political ramifications. Teachers need confidence, sensitivity and experience to be able to use attainment targets as a constructive guide to developing curriculum practices. I fear the destructive interpretations which can be made about failures to attain the required targets.

What more needs to be said about writing development? There are hundreds of ideas books on the market and various theories competing for attention. Dedicated writing teachers need to believe in a comprehensive theory of writing development which can translate into effective practice for them and their students. The work of James Britton and his colleagues in England during the 1970s, of Donald Graves in America in the 1980s, and of James Moffett over the past three decades, has undoubtedly been enormously influential in expanding our concepts about the theory and practice of writing in education. I think it is timely to review the theories and practices informing the interactive or process approach to writing development in the light of insights gained by implementing them. It should be apparent throughout this book that my own work has been influenced by an interactive, student-centred approach to writing development, and that the theoretical developments I argue for in the direction of a psychodynamic perspective are the outcome of working in an interactive way. In the light of my own teaching, research and reflections on experience, I needed to expand upon the current theories of writing development to take account of what I regard as the powerfully influential psychological processes involved in composing writing, and the dynamism inherent in such composing. It has concerned me that, where human development is represented by lines or continuums along vertical or horizontal axes (Britton *et al.* 1975), there is the implication that such development is stratified or hierarchical – as if we move beyond certain early phases in development, leaving behind their influence upon us. As you will see later, when I present a spiral concept of writing development, I believe we incorporate within us the early phases of development and expand upon them in a more fluid and dynamic way than straight lines or steps can suggest.

I would like to share some of my observations and insights with teachers of all grade levels who are curious about the complexities of writing development and who read books not so much for quick remedies to immediate problems but to engage in reflective reading as part of a global professional development.

It may be that you share with me a sense of awe at what students can do under quite trying conditions rather than a despair at what they fail to achieve. This book attempts to illuminate some of the complex issues involved in writing development and to provide some experimentally tested approaches which demonstrably made a difference to students' writing abilities, with the full knowledge that no experiment is truly replicable. The greatest wisdoms come from the students themselves. They can often express for us the best theories about teaching and learning.

A number of themes inform the structure of the following chapters. One is that students have a powerful need to symbolize themselves and their world through writing, drawing or other expressive forms. I believe they want to make their mark on the world and one of our tasks as writing teachers is to reduce the constraints that often inhibit writing development – such as a negative self-image as a writer, the frustrations of disjointed, meaningless writing experiences and premature correction of writing.

Another theme is that students demonstrate different writing abilities when they engage in real writing tasks, involving authentic dialogue with peers, from those we routinely see in most school and test writing. A third theme is that we must find ways to engage students' tacit abilities to express themselves and their connections with the world of knowledge and experience, because, as teachers of writing, we will never have sufficient time, resources and energy to develop these abilities without our students' full and willing engagement in the task. We can only guide, facilitate, model effective writing practices and processes and provide positive and constructive responses to writing. We cannot, and should not, find the words or provide the meanings. That would rob writing of its intrinsically self-important role – its capacity to engage writers in a discovery and reflection of the self as an individual and in relationship with others.

A fourth and final theme is that teachers must have a theory and philosophy of writing development. That theory provides guidelines for both the teacher and the student as to the features of language, thinking and creativity which constitute writing development, while the philosophy provides guidelines to the desirable processes and outcomes of a truly integrated and developmentally sound writing programme.

1 A psychodynamic approach to writing development

A psychodynamic approach to writing development rests on the understanding that, just as small children develop speech in a social environment in which they hear spoken language, attempt to use it themselves, receive responses to their efforts and recognize unconsciously how language can function for them, so too writing development is best promoted within a similarly engaging and dynamic environment. In such an environment writers engage with other writers and readers (including teachers) and feel valued for their expressiveness and explorations with language. One of the long-lasting and positive effects of the work of researchers/teachers like James Britton, James Moffett, Janet Emig, George Kelly, Andrew Wilkinson and others, all whom I would regard as working in an interactive and implicitly psychodynamic model, is the ready acceptance among many English teachers of the complexity of influences upon students' writing development.

Inherent in the psychodynamic model is an interest in the mind of the writer at work, not just an interest in the texts they produce, revealing as they can be. We now recognize the value of encouraging students to engage in exploratory, tentative, self-directed writing experiences as precursors to or alongside more formal, other-directed writing experiences. Later on I argue more fully that the former kinds of writing provide a developmental spring for the latter – not just as part of the cognitive aspect of writing development but for the power-ful psychological benefits which accrue from feeling centred in one's own exploratory writing and focusing on one's expressive needs.

I think we need to give more attention to the psychological aspects of writing development, for example, to the role of self-esteem and self-concept as a learner and a writer, and to the place of writing in developing and maintaining aspects of personal identity. It is difficult to continue writing unless there are intrinsic rewards in the process. It can be pleasurable, self-developing and creative if our expressive, communicative needs are the primary motivation to write. That motivation does not preclude writing in diverse ways; it simply, and essentially, underpins the process of developing writing abilities. While the function and audience categories developed by Britton *et al.*(1975) provided important conceptual frameworks in their time, I think our understanding of writing development can be further enhanced by a more dynamic model which attempts to integrate writers with their audiences, purposes and psychological, expressive needs. I will put forward such a model shortly. The psychodynamic theory of writing development outlined here blends a number of insights from psycholinguistics and psychotherapy because both approaches to human development stress, in different ways, the potential of the individual to develop expressive abilities and insight through interaction with significant others. The work of Carl Rogers and the self-psychologist/analyst Heinz Kohut also inform this point of view.

The interplay between self and society in developing the mind

Once a small child learns the denotation of words, part of the process of socialization is in train. The child accepts certain socially and culturally endorsed meanings of the words, simultaneously learning that the functional aspects of those words can be negotiated. 'Yes' and 'No' can denote a clear affirmation or negative, until varying tones of voice indicate their shades of meaning, or their potential for negotiation. In early exchanges with a parent even the very small child recognizes intuitively, or from experience, that even simple words can vary in meaning depending on the speaker and the context.

The connotations of many words are obviously highly subjective and the life-long process of literacy development involves continuous reshaping of words and their meanings as we engage in dialogues with ourself, with others and with the multitude of print and non-print symbolizations of meanings. To add to the complexity of the development of a self and of literacy ability, unconscious processes also play their part in the development and the repression of meaning. This is evident when different people share their interpretations of poems or novels. Undoubtedly we are all influenced in our reading, writing, speaking and listening by our conscious, subconscious and unconscious associations with various words and symbols – it is this that makes encounters with texts and with others such an engaging and potentially self-patterning experience. By self-patterning I mean those deeply felt language experiences in which we struggle to find words to structure our thinking and feeling.

When the struggle is successful and we create a satisfactory, albeit reworkable, pattern to reflect what previously had been rather visceral and unformulated, there can be a strong sense of the self being patterned by the struggle too. We can experience ourselves as capable of symbolizing our perceptions and feelings. Our self-concept can include a self able to create and re-create experiences. That in turn can become an energizing, self-mobilizing experience. Like the kid on a bike for the first time calling, 'Look, Mum, I can do it!', we can enjoy that synthesis of conscious and tacit abilities which results in mastery of an ability. For a moving, if harrowing account of one woman's struggle to find herself, and liberate herself, through her expressive, exploratory language in psychoanalysis, read Marie Cardinal's *The Words to Say It* (1984).

Language enables us to receive the knowledge of the culture and the society, and it invites us to shape that knowledge in paradoxical ways – paradoxical because there is a fine balance to be maintained between retaining connectedness with the society while still exploring the boundaries and potential of the connecting points. The metaphors of poetry can test the limits, but, if successful, they can also extend those limits – just as can innovative scientific theories. One might even argue that the struggle to recognize and to experiment with societies' limitations and potentials through the experience of early language learning has a powerfully unconscious influence upon the individual's self-identity. As an individual develops a conscious awareness of how language functions and can be structured, a feeling of empowerment, of appropriate self-importance and of connectedness with society and with others can be experienced. No matter how successful one is in other life endeavours, an inability to master language and to engage in effective spoken and written discourse can be humiliating and self-defeating. The struggle and the challenge to make sense of the world and of our individual place in its collective enterprises are both fraught with defeats and rich with rewards. Indeed it is a paradoxical human dilemma dependent for its resolution on the willingness of parents, teachers and significant others to encourage language learners to engage in a variety of discourse experiences in order to create a sense of oneself as significant within the relatively undifferentiated collectiveness of society.

A dynamic approach to language learning

A dynamic approach to language learning which underpins a psychodynamic theory is active, expressive, student centred, creative and imaginative, and may involve other symbolic activities like drawing, movement, drama, model-making and play activities, alone and with others. Ideally such an approach will not necessarily become less creative and more formal as students move up the secondary school but will continue to encourage the development of both creative and analytic abilities. In a dynamic and interactive learning classroom the teacher will encourage exploration and self-expression through reading, writing, speaking and listening in the belief that students have the ability and the need to make sense of their world through experiences in a range of discourses. At the same time the teacher will have a well-developed working model of what constitutes development in literacy and will be able to structure language tasks in ways which promote that development. The teacher will also be a model of a well-integrated, creative and analytic mind.

It is generally not acknowledged that the interactive classroom can provide the teacher, as well as the students, with opportunities for imaginative explorations of texts and human interactions, together with opportunities for self-reflection and cognitive development. The teacher's responsibility is to structure developmental language activities which increase the students' language awareness and language use, to provide an adult, responsive, constructive audience for their language work, along with the audiences provided by their peers, and to clarify with them the kinds of thinking, language and creative abilities they may have demonstrated in their work. The teacher needs to be engaged with students some times and appropriately disengaged other times in order to analyse sensitively what is happening in the classroom and what needs restructuring. Such a balanced, demanding role for the teacher requires, at the very least, insight, well-developed personal language skills, empathy, flexibility and a capacity to engage students in analysing classroom interactions. One of the many advantages of an interactive classroom, however, is that the teacher can involve students in perceiving, analysing, reflecting and commenting upon that they hear, see, feel and think as they engage in classroom activities. The classroom can become a workshop for real life and a safe environment for experimentation and risk-taking. This suggests, of course, that the classroom relationships are healthy, positive and self-affirming. If they are not, then the teacher will need to work on understanding the dynamics of that class and try to establish a good working environment of trust and self-respect. Again this can be done through language, through reading, through journal writing and through any number of language activities which involve self-expression and promote self-understanding.

For all the overwhelming demands placed on teachers, and especially English teachers, there is one distinct advantage enjoyed by English teachers: the content of lessons can be the thoughts, feelings, ambivalences, fears, hopes and even regressions of the students themselves. When we add literature to the already present human content of our lessons, we have the potential for highly dynamic and creative language, literature, and life work. It goes almost without saying that teachers who do not thoroughly enjoy intense relationships with others – that is, relationships which involve a degree of self-disclosure, a large measure of trust and a certain amount of risk-taking, as in an interactive language classroom, and teachers who do not enjoy working out how the world, themselves and other people tick, are probably not going to be very effective language teachers. A large measure of insatiable curiosity, good humour and self-reflection, and the ability to endure delayed gratification (language development is a very slow process) are important qualities for interactive language teachers – qualities similar to those needed for good parenting which is so important in early language development. The comparison is important because yet another quality teachers and parents need in order to be effective is the capacity for authentic relationships, relationships in which individuals can be appropriately expressive and exploratory.

Authentic writing

It is difficult to define authentic writing. It is not just expressive writing; some so-called expressive writing can sound very phoney and some highly transactional writing can sound very authentic. The best explanation I can offer is that it is writing which emanates from a writer's search for meaning – as distinct from perfunctory writing which simply records information or meets some externally imposed demands. Readers of authentic writing should feel they are reading verbalizations which primarily meet the needs of the writer. That is, authentic writers need not be audience unaware, but their primary focus will be on expressing, communicating and maybe working through some view of the world, or some exploration of an idea or issue. In that kind of composing process writers feel enhanced, as possibly do their readers. It can sometimes be difficult to determine the authenticity of writing but it becomes easier with experience, particularly for teachers who are familiar with their students writers. The value of talking and thinking about it is that we can reflect on our own authentic writing experiences and develop an ear and eye for it in our students' writing. At the simplest level, authentic writing sounds genuine. Contrived writing sounds phoney. Ability to sub-text discourse, or to read between the lines helps us to recognize authentic language. One of the best examples of authentic and inauthentic language can be heard from sub-texting the speeches of Regan, Goneril and Cordelia in reply to King Lear in the first scene of the play, *King Lear*. Analyses of grammar alone will not reveal the authentic and the inauthentic. We need to apply our own intuitions and world knowledge to the interpretative task, something even small children are skilled at doing.

James Moffet (1981a) discusses the role of authentic writing in discourse development and analyses his own development as a writer in these terms. It is illuminating to read his own professional work from *Teaching the Universe of Discourse* (1968) through to *Coming on Center* (1981a) in light of the changes in his writing voice over that time. It is easier to witness students being authentic in their expression and their symbolization in their early school years than it is in secondary schools. The pressure to conform to social expectations and indeed peer pressures to conformity in adolescent years work against the development of individuality. Conversely, such pressures can lead some individuals to seek expression through their writing. There is also an often well-founded fear that individuality will not be endorsed in public examinations of written expression, in spite of the mandates of well-intentioned syllabuses, and it requires a degree of self-confidence and articulateness to express one's individuality in convention-ally valued ways. One of the greatest challenges of life is to develop personal authenticity and integrity in societies which are often threatened by, mystified by and hostile to individual development. Again, interactive language teachers will need a deeply felt belief in the value of the individual, and in the value of language experiences to develop individuals' potential in order to tolerate the many defeats we experience in undertaking this kind of work.

Interactive language work is no soft option. Language development is notoriously slow to develop. From the experience of working on a four-year longitudinal writing-research project, I can acknowledge the frustration and bewilderment I experienced in trying to provide some positive developmental experiences for some of the experimental students. One student, John, baffled me completely, even though he stayed with the intervention writing[1] programme until the end and seemed to like coming to the sessions. But the defeats need not negate the theoretical base of an interactive language approach. Rather they can provide a challenge to seek a further refinement of that theory: a challenge to reach the person so well defended against possible language failure that expression and communication is kept to a minimum. By the end of four years with John (see page 106), his communication with me was little more than an occasional greeting, a sigh, a groan or a shy, eyes-averted smile. Yet John had written in one of his few extended written pieces following a pre-writing concentration exercise, in early Year 7[2], 'Its marvellous what the mine[sic] can see'. The ellipsis of 'mind' and 'mine', or the Freudian slip, if you like, is powerfully evocative.

John needed a sustained once-daily session with a writing teacher who could provide support, positive mirroring, exploratory writing experiences and interesting reading materials. He could have been helped, I think, with a more intensive reading and writing programme than I could provide with my once-a-fortnight visits. He needed more of the self-enhancing experiences which made him marvel at his own mind (or mine of hidden treasures, as his 'mistake' might suggest). With a reluctant student like John it takes enormous energy and patience to discover what attracts and holds his interest. School certainly doesn't.

What is useful to us as teachers is the acknowledgement implicit in a valuing of authentic writing, of the role writing can play in self-development and self-reflection when the writer is truly centred in the writing experience. I develop an argument through this book that such self-centredness, in a psychologically sound sense, is a crucial spring for the development of other-awareness.

Of course many teachers feel there is insufficient time in the secondary schools, at least, to allow students to develop their own authentic writing voice, and the same teachers may feel that such a voice will not be valued in public examinations. On the issue of the time factor, moves to develop Kindergarten to Year 12 perspectives on writing development, perspectives officially recognized in New South Wales, give positive endorsement to the kinds of interactive writing methods in which authentic writing can flourish. Furthermore, public-examination questions, at least in English, are now seeking more overtly students' self-expression, together with some measure of critical judgement. Many experienced examiners and teachers can pick out phoney responses or those formulated mainly in teachers' language. For whatever reasons, possibly because they are not in touch with their own expressiveness, some teachers do lack the faith or time to allow students to develop their own world view and their responses to literature through the use of their own language. The most compelling reason for encouraging authentic writing is that it centres students within their own learning experiences, it releases tacit language and thinking abilities which continue to develop long after the writing lessons have finished, and it enables students to experience a positive sense of themselves as writers and learners.

A sad reflection on modern education was expressed by one of my experimental students, writing in response to a focused-concentration exercise in her final year of primary school. She wrote, 'This is the first time I knew what I could think.' In the concentration exercise all she had been asked to do was remain still and quiet, eyes closed, sitting on the floor in the classroom with the other fifteen students, watching what went on in her mind. Several of her classmates who had engaged in that activity also wrote of their surprise and delight in discovering the richness of their own memories, reflections and stored experiences. For all that the exercise was successful, it does take a certain amount of unshakable faith in students' abilities to believe that such open-ended, expressive, personalized experiences will be worthwhile. When they are so, the students' responses are usually spontaneously affirming. With some hesitation, because it is so subjective a response, I will also report that, when the students were truly concentrating during that exercise, there was an atmosphere in the room of remarkable calmness, intensity and concentration. Something important was going on and I think it had to do with the students' self-discoveries. It was quite inspiring.

The writing which followed the concentration exercise was effortless, engaging and revealing. Significantly, when students had had sufficient experience of that kind of exercise and the subsequent writing, they wanted to move to writing which was more 'other-directed', as I will discuss later on.

The role of the unconscious in writing

There is another aspect of that kind of writing exercise described above which needs some explanation: the role of unconscious processes in writing development. One of the ways we can encourage unconscious forces to surface, not that they are not operating upon us all the time, is to engage in contemplative thought in which attention upon external stimuli is shifted towards attention upon internal stimuli. Writers and thinkers with their attention set upon writing and its processes can often become more aware of the unconscious influences upon those processes when they engage in reflections on their writing and thinking. These reflections can be expressed through and become part of a metalanguage, or language to describe composing processes. I think that the value of being in touch with unconscious influences, both positive and negative ones, such as repressed memories of deflating comments, or ego-boosting ones, which might have been made on one's efforts in the past, is that such awareness can engage the co-operation of the unconscious in the composing process. The more we are in touch with, and in tune with the internal influences upon composing processes, the more able we are to be enhanced rather than overwhelmed by them. Because our unconscious memories have been repressed, often for good reason, they are unlikely to be revealed in a positive way unless the context is non-threatening and potentially developmental.

Of course, as Freud's analysis of jokes and slips of the tongue revealed, often our unconscious revelations can be both threatening and revealing. I argue here that the ability to write authentically, to decentre and to see the world in increasingly differentiated ways, underpins all writing development. The experience of writing can help one to see the world in increasingly more complex ways, just as writing can also reflect that ability. In psychodynamic terms, writing development is a personalized, energized interplay between process and product. That is what underpins the adage, 'you learn to write by writing'. As students begin to decentre and are able to write for audiences beyond themselves and about subjects beyond the here and now, it is important that their writing retains its personalized base.

Even the most complex ideas like the speculations of ground-breaking theories or the metaphoric elaborations of poetry can be voiced in authentic ways. The authentic writer will be closely in touch with the creativity of the enterprise and sensitive, attuned readers of that writing will recognize that. Often such speculations or elaborations have involved a deep working through of the writer's perceptions and ideas so the authentic voice underpins the communication. Where writers are simply repeating others' ideas, there is every likelihood that the writing will sound superficial and even disintegrated. Obviously we all use communities of vocabulary and well recognized syntactic structures, but the variability of language is such that there is always scope for individual expressiveness and style. Authentic writing can be self-generating, in several senses of the term: you can start it on your own, it can generate a sense of your self as 'self-starting' and it can energize a sense of self.

Students with even a relatively brief experience of authentic writing begin to think of themselves as writers, and to store up, even unconsciously, experiences which will become part of their further writing. They become more conscious, too, of the conventions of writing, and keen to match those conventions. Journal writing and writing to peers offer a form of dialogue with self and others which has a recursive effect; the act of writing, while simultaneously visualizing the audience for the writing, even if it is only oneself, activates the writer's writing voice. That is, the writer senses that the writing has an ultimate audience. Writing is also self-generating in that as one writes authentically, and with an integrity which brings together formerly disparate thoughts and images, the writer's self expands to include an image of self-as-writer. There is a lively interplay between self as individual, self as communicator and self as symbolizer. This in itself can create a notion of the complexity of one's self and of one's capacity to engage in different, though complementary, expressive roles.

Writers as self-monitors

Humans constantly monitor their self-perceptions as successful or unsuccessful achievers of certain tasks. We all carry images of ourselves as good or bad performers of a wide range of skills. Clearly the skilled performance of some tasks is highly rewarded, materially and in other ways. Unfortunately writing is most highly esteemed as a means to an end – a high grade in examinations for school success and possibly tertiary-education entrance. Writing is too rarely esteemed for the intrinsically rewarding benefits it can confer on those who experience its self-developing and self-affirming potential. Assessment and monitoring practices like those advocated by Brian Johnston (1987) which involve writers in determining their own progress are infinitely more conducive to continued writing than examination-type assessments which rarely provide constructive feedback.

For too long writing abilities of a narrow, transactional kind have been regarded as possible evidence of schools' and teachers' success or failure in preparing students for life after school. The over-heavy reliance on teacher-dictated notes which still dominates many senior school classrooms can be explained only by a lack of faith in students' abilities to make sense of information and of their learning experiences through their own reflections and their engagements with reading, writing and related discourse experiences.

The lack of time devoted to sustained composition and related language experiences in secondary schools especially, suggests a need for well-integrated, realistic and informed writing programmes with a Kindergarten to Year 12 perspective. A comprehensive theory of writing development should underpin such programmes and assessment procedures and monitoring practices should be consistent with such a theory. Ideally that theory will reflect the belief that students need to make their mark on the world, and to formulate their own life experiences through their self-expression and self-symbolization as writers.

I suspect that if more teachers themselves had enjoyed writing experiences which gave them as much joy as small children experience when they symbolize through drawing, craft, play and early writing, this argument would not even need to be articulated. If, as the anatomist J. Z. Young (1978) postulates, in a frustratingly brief argument, that part of the brain is programmed to write, much human potential is thwarted if opportunities are not provided for the development of that programme within individuals. Generally the focus is upon the need for writing to communicate with an audience – usually someone external to the writer, but I want to argue both implicitly and explicitly throughout this book that a primary reason for writing can be to communicate with the self in order to develop the self. The self is variously dependent, independent and interdependent, and it is capable of seeking from the environment the means of its own physical, emotional and social nourishment. When the basic needs for physical survival have been satisfied, the need to engage in some kind of mirroring experiences with significant others is generally expressed. Mirroring experiences in this metaphoric sense, are those experiences which allow us to sense ourselves or see ourselves reflected in the responses of others. So important are they that small infants can fail to thrive, even when physical nourishment is readily available, unless they also experience endorsement or mirroring from a significant other in forms of eye-gazing, communicative sounds and close physical contact. We experience a sense of ourselves through our reciprocal engagements with others, and through various forms of self-expression like dance, music, art and writing. I would argue that what is unique to writing is its capacity to symbolize and to communicate extremely well-differentiated forms of thought and feeling. By this I mean we can structure language in ways which sensitively and accurately reflect the thought and feeling we wish to express. The words we choose, the genre, the style, the format, the tone of voice and so on, orchestrate that symbolization.

In essence, the arguments informing this book acknowledge that, although society has granted special status to writing abilities in the emphasis given to the evidence of those abilities in public examinations, aspects of that emphasis have been misplaced and misguided. Writing is valuable as a means of recording information and reflecting individuals' thoughts, but its greatest value to individuals is in the capacity of composing processes to integrate and express some of the thoughts, feelings and impressions which flow through the human mind, often in previously unformulated and undifferentiated forms. In particular, the capacity for authentic writing to generate further thought in both the writer and its readers attests to its basic creativity and to its self-perpetuating nature. Writers who feel centred in their own writing need relatively little encouragement to continue – sometimes little more than the peripheral attention of an endorsing audience – like the small child absorbed in a task who still likes to know such an audience is within earshot. Such is the interplay between independence, dependence and interdependence in symbolization activities. As such an activity writing allows an interplay between the individual mind and the society of which it is a part so that both may be transformed and enhanced by the process.

Self-esteem, self-concept and self-disclosure in writing

While there is obvious tacit belief in the value of students' positive self-esteem in language learning, and one of the most influential books on English education, *Growth through English* (Dixon 1975), emphasized the individual in literacy development, little systematic work has been done on the role of self-esteem in that development. Nor has much been done to analyse the nature of the relationships between teachers and their students in the process. There is some implicit evidence in the case study approaches reported by Emig (1971), Graves (1983) and Atwell (1987), and an acknowledgement of the importance of affective development in Wilkinson's (1986) work. Most empathic teachers would believe that their positive encouragement of students, together with sound modelling of writing practices, would benefit students' writing development, but there is scant detailed work on the complexities of dynamics in an interactive language classroom. Empirical research usually focuses on end results, obviously, yet teachers know there are often key moments in a classroom when change is perceptible, if even fleetingly. Some of the examples given throughout this book record such moments.

Theory in practice

My own interest in authentic writing and the role of self-esteem intensified during the four years I worked on the writing intervention project referred to throughout this book. After a period of time writing, following concentration exercises, free-association writing and writing activities where the primary audience was the self and the main purpose for the writing was self-expression and self-discovery, the experimental writers signalled their need for a change in direction. They had had enough experience of mainly self-centred work and they asked if they could exchange letters with the students in the parallel experimental group in another school. On reflection, this was a very natural development. When we have had enough time working from within ourselves, we usually want to share or connect with others. In response to the students' request, I paired a writer in one school, quite arbitrarily, with another experimental writer in the parallel school. The writers had to introduce themselves to their writing partners and establish a relationship through their letters. There was enthusiasm for the task, and a certain amount of excitement and apprehension – such as one might experience in certain new tasks. This kind of writing was very different to the kinds of writing going on in the students' regular classrooms. Here was a real audience and the potential for a continuing relationship through writing. I became the courier taking the letters between the group in each school. Sometimes the students would be waiting at the school gate for my arrival with the letters. It was very gratifying to be so enthusiastically welcomed – if only for the letters I carried!

While I was pleased that this method was so engaging and intrinsically worthwhile for the students, I was temporarily somewhat concerned about making sense of this development in terms of current writing-development theory and my own research plan. Counteracting my concern was a belief that, as the letter writing was a student initiative and stimulated such a responsive flow of writing, it must have some significant implications for writing-development theory. Hence my interest in the psychological factors influencing such development.

The challenge in acting as a teacher-researcher was to analyse those contexts as both participant and observer, and to analyse the students' letters. The students were quite happy to share the letters with me once they had read them. My role in the writing sessions during this letter-writing exchange was to be empathic and constructively helpful. I would suggest content for the letters or interpret meaning where there was some ambiguity in expression. When I read these letters after a period of about six months of exchanges, I was impressed with the overwhelming concentration in the earlier letters in particular, on what I termed 'self-esteem comments'; that is, comments which functioned to endorse the self-esteem of the writing partner or to seek endorsement from him/her. For example, students wrote,

I've liked your letter very much and your letter never bored me a bit. I just hoped I never bored you.

Sorry my writing is messy but I am interested in you and have so many questions.

I'm very pleased that you have sent a letter. I enjoyed reading your letter.

I don't think you are a show off because talking about yourself is the way to find out about others.

Without exception the experimental writers all made several self-esteem comments in their early letters. The total number of comments in the first six letters ranged from three for one writer to twenty-two for another. When you think about it, the establishment of a positive relationship is usually based on some mutual liking or shared esteem, or upon some expectation of intrinsic rewards. These students transferred into this particular discourse context their understanding of relationships gained from past experience and intuition. It should not even be remarkable that they did so, except that most classroom situations do not encourage that particular kind of relationship or its possible continuity. The students in this letter exchange had to establish and maintain their relationship with their partner solely through writing; consequently there is evidence in their letters of each of their relating skills, and of their acknowledged interdependence. I exemplify this point through the case studies later.

It is unlikely that a teacher will be able to elicit this kind of evidence without the stimulus of a genuine peer audience such as the letter-writing exchange provided. I believe that these students were intuitively aware of an aspect of writing development which we as teachers have lost sight of. If, even as adult writers, we were to analyse our own writing processes, it would be unlikely that we would be in touch with this particular aspect of self-esteem in writing, unless we also engaged in that particular task – writing to an unknown peer with whom we hoped to continue a writing relationship. If students can reveal spontaneously the importance of self-esteem in establishing relationships and in accomplishing certain writing tasks, clearly we need to pay more attention to the messages they give us. Although I have commented mainly on the overtly self-endorsing or other-endorsing comments, the receipt of an authentic communication through a letter from a writing partner was, in itself, a positive, mirroring experience for the writers. The reciprocity of the exchange meant that both partners had to co-operate to maintain it, and for the less able writers this was often quite a challenge.

Robyn, for example, was a keen but rather laboured writer. She took a while to warm to the task but then did not want to stop, especially if the topic was intrinsically interesting to her. She reassured her writing partner: 'I don't think you are a show off because talking about yourself is the way to find out about others.'

Even Shane, who ranked with John (see case study, page 105) as a most reluctant writer, knew how to engage his writing partner's interest: 'I'm very pleased that you have sent a letter. I enjoyed reading your letter.'

All too rarely do teachers and students engage in that kind of exchange. The role relationships between teachers and students discourage mutuality but those roles can change. As you will see in the case study of Anna and Jane, the empathic sharing of personal issues between students can be extremely valuable for their emotional and cognitive development. They can begin to see issues from different points of view while relating to and learning from each other. Obviously this can happen in their conversations, in journal writing and other reflective writing, as well as in a pen friendship. Clearly trust and some promise of continuity in a penfriend relationship are important. I think it was also important in the letter-writing exchange that the students had a feeling of space to explore their relationships through their letters and a degree of distance in that they were highly unlikely to meet their writing partner face to face. In such circumstances self-disclosure could be risked.

The self-esteem issue became more complex and revealing in the case of the writing partners Jane and Anna. Their relationships, which was developed solely through their exchange of letters, involved many significant changes in focus and intensity throughout that exchange. Their ability to negotiate their relationship through writing and to confront and resolve conflicts between them attests to an important aspect of writing development which is largely neglected in school contexts; the potential for socially engaging, mutually beneficial writing between peers to develop their self-awareness together with their awareness of others.

Summary

- A psychodynamic theory of writing development is informed by an awareness of the psychological influences upon writers' processes and products and implemented through authentic writing and interactive language experiences.
- Psychological influences include writers' self-concept, self-disclosures, relating abilities and the role of the unconscious.
- Authentic writing, decentring and increased differentiation in thought and language underpin writing development.
- The development of authentic writing demands complex abilities of the teacher.
- Authentic writing enhances both writers and readers, contributing significantly to their self-development.

Notes

1 Throughout the book the term 'intervention writing', and variations of the term, are used to describe the author's specifically designed writing programme. Selected students were withdrawn from their regular classrooms to undertake writing activities

with the author which were not part of their usual classroom work. These activities could well have been part of a regular English classroom and, indeed, are endorsed in the English Curriculum guidelines appropriate for the schools used in the research project. See Appendix A for further details.

2 In Australia children start formal schooling at about 5 years old when they enter kindergarten class in primary (elementary) school (Year K). They then complete (school) Years 1–6 in primary school before moving into high school (sometimes called secondary school) for (school) Years 7–12.

The students involved in this project were in their final year of primary school (Year 6) when the project started and at the end of Year 9 when it was completed. They were about 11 years old at the start of the project and about 14 at its completion.

2 Writing development as a metaphoric spiral

I hope it is clear from the first chapter that this book has its genesis in a developmental view of writing as a process involving a complex of linguistic, cognitive and psychological factors. Such a view has theoretical underpinnings which draw upon research and theory in a number of related disciplines. I will outline some of the major influences on the book's conception, including contributing theories and insights gained from the study I undertook to test an hypothesis about interactive writing experiences. I will also offer a tentative speculation about relevant psychological influences upon writing development which I believe need further investigation.

In an attempt to conceptualize writing development in a figurative way which both integrates relevant theory and may possibly provide a model for teachers concerned about long-term writing development, I will demonstrate and explain my own concept of writing development visualized as a metaphoric spiral (fig. 2.1).

I regard the model as a psychodynamic one because it is based on a concept of writing development as resulting from an active engagement between the writer's psyche (a cognitive and psychological entity) and environment, including significant others.

What I suggest here is a representation of development in writing abilities (and other literacy development) which I think centres that development within the individual. It suggests a dynamic potential for development in which the self can expand through the process of internalizing increasingly more differentiated forms of language use.

The spiral model

The ribs

The ribs of the cone represent various kinds of language found in the universe of discourse. I have used the now familiar terms expressive, transactional and poetic

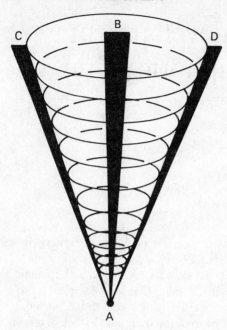

A = Core self
B = Expressive self incorporating expressive discourse (spoken and written)
C = Transactional discourse (spoken and written)
D = Poetic discourse (spoken and written)

Figure 2.1 Spiral model of psychodynamic discourse development

language. While I would want to retain expressive language at the heart of the development process, the other ribs could represent all kinds of discourse, both spoken and written. The ribs stand for the 'givens' in a language environment – the broad categories of language functions one is likely to encounter in writing and speech. The ribs themselves enlarge as the spiral expands, suggesting the increasingly more complex and differentiated forms of the language functions one can recognize and internalize in the process of development.

The revolving spring

The core of the spiral is a revolving spring starting at point A, the core self. From the core self develops the expressive self which has a capacity to engage in all kinds of active or receptive, reading, speaking, writing and listening activities. In early childhood, the spring is coiled down hard, with the potential to grow, and surrounded by different forms of language, including various audiences and purposes. As the spring uncoils, it also rotates around these different forms, modes or functions, internalizing them when ready and, if the process is truly developmental, forever moving upwards and outwards. The spring is intended to suggest self-contained energy, the centre of which is the fusing of the spring within the cone of potential experience. As the self-writer develops, he/she is able to perceive, use and internalize increasingly more complex discourse functions. Accordingly, the self incorporates discourse experiences and thereby grows.

If we imagine the spring as a core self with the capacity to internalize and integrate discourse experiences, then we can visualize the self-centred, self-generating and self-reflective nature of that developmental process. Self-centred here means a self which centres the process and has a capacity for continued expansion as it integrates experiences with the social, material and symbolic world.

Others as mirroring audiences

Where are adults, teachers and audiences in this seemingly independent process? They are represented as reflecting mirrors within the cone. They are essential to the process not only for their ability to mirror writers (and speakers) back to themselves but because they can also mirror or provide models of the kinds of developmental language experiences essential for individuals' growth. They can be present for the writer as what Kohut (1984) calls a 'twin self', and they can constructively help writers to match their discourse intentions with audience expectations. Sometimes the role of the constructive editor/audience can be to help the writer to sharpen the image between the self and the target audience – maybe removing some metaphoric smudges from the glass on the mirror – other times the role can be simply to reflect back to the writer a sense of self-as-writer. The self is never a completely independent being, particularly in language development which is so powerfully mediated by interpersonal and social relationships.

Others as empathic audiences

Essentially the role of the audience or significant other in this model is to enhance the developmental process by being empathic with the self-writer's intentions and achievements so that he/she can smoothly internalize a sense of appropriate audiences, and constructive in mirroring increasingly more complex audiences and functions. Where audiences are mainly non-responsive, such as readers of a book like this, any developmental aspect for the writer has to come from the imagined interplay between herself and her projected sense of that audience; an interplay dependent on previously internalized experiences and a capacity for hypothesizing readers' expectations.

The basic function of the metaphoric spiral is to symbolize the dynamic and potentially developmental interplay between the writer and the external world of audiences and discourse forms. The writer is conceived as an expressive self with a capacity for infinite development, if that development is centred within the self and if there are opportunities for encounters with increasingly more differentiated discourse forms, and more complex audiences.

The coil of the spiral which moves up and out symbolizes the self-generating capacity of the self-writer engaged in this active process of reaching out and up, using and engaging with written and spoken language and being mirrored by responsive audiences.

Obviously this model is idealized, as are most conceptualizations of human development. True development involves regressions which might be visualized here as faint spirals where the self-writer fails to effectively engage with certain discourse forms for whatever reasons. It could be a 'power failure' within the self where lack of involvement short-circuited the encounter. It could be that the writer is looking through a glass too darkly. This is where the attuned/empathic audience, be it adult, teacher or peer, can play an important role in enabling writers to match their discourse intentions with society's expectations, while still engaging an expressive experience. The empathic audience/reader also has to have the ability to increase his/her expectations of writers realistically, sensitively and constructively.

In this model the role of the audience/reader is more dynamic than the role of discourse forms. The audience has a close relationship with the writer in reflecting different discourse forms (this could be, in practical terms, heading the writer towards appropriate models of writing) and in responding to the writer. I want to emphasize that peer audiences can be as effective, sometimes more so, than adult audiences, and that the primary role of the audience is to be there for the writer. From a position of attunement and empathy constructive help and direction help can be given and received. Eventually, mature writers become less dependent upon the mirroring of external audiences, never entirely so, of course, so at the top of this spiral the spring might move beyond the reflecting audiences. This is to indicate that to a large extent a range of audiences could have been internalized within the writer's mind.

What I have tried to do with this model is represent in a dynamic way my own conceptualization of writing development. The model is more dynamic than I first thought in that I find myself regularly revising it. I hope my readers do the same.

Background to the development of the metaphoric spiral

I have been influenced here by the work of Moffett, Vygotsky, Luria, Britton and others and I have attempted to elaborate a working model of writing development which acknowledges the integrating power of inner speech and authentic writing. In this model, self-expression and self-development become dynamic forces in the writers' willingness to continue writing. They do so because they see themselves reflected in their writing. The psychological processes of self-knowledge and self-development inherent in this model in turn increase the writer's awareness of others and their external world. That is, a continuity can occur between knowing self and knowing others.

Central to this model and to the practices undertaken in the writing study described throughout the book is a belief in the tacit power[1] of expressive and authentic writing, to promote writing development through self-symbolization.

That is, the individual writers have the capacity to develop the cognitive and linguistic abilities central to writing development, provided they have sufficient access to language resources within their environment to internalize discourse patterns, and responsive audiences at particular times. A crucial factor is the writer's sense of self as a writer. That is the spring central to this psychodynamic model. I made reference earlier to the writer's psyche as a cognitive and psychological entity. I would like now to elaborate further upon the cognitive aspect of the psyche engaged in writing development, with respect to the role of inner speech and thinking.

Inner speech, thinking and writing

Moffett (1981b) argues that experiences involving the revision of inner speech are essential for an effective, developmental writing programme across the curriculum. He sees that the process of authentic writing involves tapping the stream of inner speech and focusing it, selecting and editing excerpts from it and ordering it according to innate abstracting faculties. He argues that what composition teachers call 'coherence', 'organization' and 'style', 'are manifestations in writing of mental functioning' (1981b: 14–15). Thus he makes a parallel between writing, or composing words on paper, and composing the mind. It may help to consider the origins of the concept of inner speech in the child's mental development. Piaget (1959) Vygotsky (1962) and Moffett (1981a) are our main sources for discussions on the role of inner speech. There were differences in detail between Vygotsky and Piaget about the nature of inner speech (see Vygotsky 1962), but for our purposes, Vygotsky's elaboration of that nature is important in understanding the interrelationship between writing, thinking and learning, and in understanding the attention given to inner speech in the writing-intervention programme described in this book.

Vygotsky developed Piaget's view (1959) about inner speech, socialized speech and the development of logic. He argued that 'the child's intellectual growth is contingent on his mastering of the social means of thought, that is, language' (Vygotsky, 1962: 51). His experimental work on concept development, based on a detailed study of the work of the child from early language development onwards, forms the basis for his argument that concept-formation involving association, attention, imagery and inference is insufficient without the use of 'the sign, or word, as the means by which we direct our mental operations, control their course, and channel them toward the solution of the problem confronting us'. (Vygotsky 1962: 58).

To Vygotsky concept development is an evolutionary process involving shifts in the child's understanding of a word's meaning as the word is encountered and used. The word fixes the constellations of images, associations and sensory responses to a thought and so takes on both a universal and a personal meaning. Central to a relationship between word and thought is a differentiation between inner and external speech. Inner speech is not the same as external speech but it is a function in itself. It remains like speech in that it is thought connected with words, but 'where thought is embodied in words in external speech, in inner speech words die as they bring forth thought. Inner speech is to a large extent thinking in pure meanings. It is a dynamic, shifting, unstable thing, fluttering between word and thought, the two more or less stable, more or less firmly delineated components of verbal thought' (Vygotsky 1962: 149).

The distinction between external speech, inner speech and thought is important because it shows how student talk and student writing allow for an interplay between thoughts, words and meanings. Concept development depends upon such creative transitions. The fullness of individual expressiveness and the development of consciousness depend on the interplay of thought and language:

'Words play a central part not only in the development of thought but in the historical growth of consciousness as a whole. A word is a microcosm of human consciousness.' (ibid: 153).

Vygotsky's (1962) exploration of the dialectical interrelationship of thought and language has implications for an understanding of the writing process. He argues that inner speech develops when the child takes over external speech from those around him and discovers the value of talking for himself. When written language is the final outcome of the movement from thought in inner speech to its expression in outer speech, then the self-directed inner speech has to be deliberately structured. To be intelligible to others, the predicative, idiomatic structure of inner speech has to be dynamically processed and syntactically structured. Vygotsky concluded that egocentric speech is a stage of development preceding inner speech, but having a genetic connection with it. It was the recognition of this genetic connection which made possible Vygotsky's investigation of the difficult area of inner speech. While both inner speech and egocentric speech fulfil intellectual functions and have a similar structure, Vygotsky observed that egocentric speech disappears at school age, when inner speech begins to develop. For a number of reasons, Vygotsky inferred that egocentric speech changes into inner speech and he used that transformation to explore the two experimentally. He disagrees with Piaget's conception that egocentric speech has no function in the child's realistic thinking and argues that it is a phenomenon of the transition from 'interpsychic to intrapsychic functioning, e.g. from the social collective activity of the child to his more individualized activity, a pattern of development common to all the higher psychological functions' (ibid: 193). I think this helps to explain why the beginning writer has to start with initial representations of spoken language.

Speech for oneself originated through an internalization of the speech of others, and through differentiation from speech for others. One of the laws of inner speech is that it omits subjects, just as it is a law of written speech that it contains subjects and predicates. As inner speech develops, predication dominates. Because children know what they are thinking, they believe that the subject and all the words connected with it can be left out. The sense of a word predominates over its meaning. Inner speech involves the essentially individualized internalization of experience. Hence its importance in the development of authentic writing, and the difficulties it poses. As children revise inner speech into written form, they have to take account of the transitions necessary in language and thought to make the meanings accessible to others. Clearly inner speech serves an important function for individuals, and that process of working through inner speech to written form allows writers to monitor what is in the mind while practising the process of transformation needed to write intelligibly. Hence, a process approach to writing development is important, not just as a method of developing writing abilities, but for the insight it allows writers into the structure of their own minds. Recall how often we have difficulty making clear to others in writing what seems clear in inner speech and thought.

Many apparent failures of communication in written language can come from failure to recognize the basic discourse structure of interrelatedness between writer, audience and subject. Somehow young writers need to recognize that writing is a way of creating from a monologue with self, a dialogue with others. By tapping inner speech in spontaneous writing, writers can witness their own language and thought and re-internalize it. Even more importantly, students' use of their own language to explore and express a concept increases their identification with it and allows them to abstract its principles, shaping them within their existing cognitive constructs. This individualized shaping process involves using words, metaphors and images in ways which help learners to construe, either rigidly or loosely, a meaning for a concept. This construing will be a dynamic process of confirming, elaborating or reducing the boundaries of the concept each time it is encountered. Luria (1969) expanded upon Vygotsky's work on inner speech, arguing that writing leads to a significant development of inner speech through the recursiveness involved in the interplay between inner speech and writing development. He contrasted the cognitive demands of both oral and written speech in order to demonstrate how writing can develop thinking, arguing that because writing requires a process of analysis and synthesis it transforms 'the sequential chains of connection into a simultaneous self-reviewing structure' (Luria 1969: 141–2). Put simply, our experiences are transformed by the process of writing about them. It has been well acknowledged that there are significant relationships among all the discourse modes (Kinneavy 1980) and between the idiosyncratic personality and world view of each writer (Bruner 1972, Moffett 1981a, 1981b). That is, the 'universe of discourse' (taken from the title of Moffett's 1968 book) is expansive enough, sufficiently well differentiated, complex and variable to provide scope for the reflections and symbolizations of vast numbers of individuals.

Psychological influences upon writing development

While the world view and personality of individual writers can be reflected in their authentic writing, the psychological influences upon writing development still deserve some attention, I believe. These influences include self-concept as a writer, self-esteem in writing, the nature of audience-mirroring available to writers, the creation of metaphors for self in writing, and the intersubjective and intrasubjective potential of the writing process. Some of these I have touched on already, others I would like to discuss now.

Self-concept as a writer

To move from the abstraction considered above, let us consider what it is that motivates some students to continue writing in all kinds of ways as part of a life style involving continuous discourse development, while others write very reluctantly and rarely. Common sense and empathy tell us that the motivated student has experienced intrinsic and possibly extrinsic rewards for writing, while the reluctant student has failed to experience sufficient rewards to continue. They can't see anything in it for them. As a salutary reminder of how effectively society and schools can thwart children's expressive and symbolizing powers as they 'progress' up the school system, consider the concentration and joyful expressiveness of pre-school, kindergarten and infant children as they paint, draw, learn letters and start writing. Then consider the anxiety, defensiveness and despair of poor writers who, for a variety of reasons, have failed to master the codes of written language and who know in their hearts the judgements society makes upon the illiterate. Success in writing can enhance individuals' self-esteem and reflect it, while failure exposes individuals to humiliation. Most of us do not continue with tasks likely to entail shame and defeat. Reluctant or poor writers need to experience some measure of self-gratification and pleasure in the act of writing, or trust in some promise of those rewards, before they will attempt to engage in it.

In a trustworthy environment some reluctant writers will willingly write and talk about their previous writing experiences, as will good writers, of course, and in so doing gain some perspective and insight into the psychological influences upon their own writing development. From my own teaching, research and clinical experiences working with both reluctant and gifted writers, I am impressed with the positive and negative influences of psychological processes upon writing development. Such is the nature of the role of self-confidence in all kinds of human endeavours that mentors, or those who believe in (or fail to believe in) our abilities, can exert a very powerful influence upon our success or otherwise. Psychoanalysts refer to this phenomenon as a positive transference. One of the very sound reasons why small children in enlightened classrooms are now encouraged to attempt writing certain words, even if they cannot spell them correctly, is because that flexibility in the attending adult's expectations signals to the child the primary importance of expressiveness above premature correctness. Children know intuitively, and from other expressive activities, that self-expression is valuable and self-enhancing, and the informed adult knows that children will, at an appropriate time, learn conventional spelling and the conventions of written discourse, if they continue to perceive psychological rewards such as a sense of achievement in so doing. If we believe that small children start writing as an extension of the process of drawing and as a more differentiated way of symbolizing the world than drawing, then we can see how writing processes can be intrinsically satisfying, expressive and potentially developmental in cognitive, linguistic and psychological terms.

The promise of publication of writing, even on a small and informal scale, involves all manner of self-presentation issues which can be positively harnessed in the interests of writing development. The writers in my research study were very keen to set out and to spell correctly their letters to their writing partners, when their pride and sense of relatedness with their partner was involved in the writing experience. Some also used drawings and other kinds of illustration as part of their writing repertoire.

One of the possible and positive side-effects of the emphasis placed on written examinations as an important criterion for school success is that many students do experience a lift in self-esteem and confidence if they can realistically perceive themselves as effective and achieving writers. Of course the converse of that can negatively influence the less able writers. A realistic balance between extrinsic and intrinsic rewards obviously benefits writing development, though problems with extrinsic rewards can arise if, for example, examination success is based on writers' ability simply to regurgitate another's point of view, thereby reinforcing artificiality and superficiality in writing. Such writing may still be rewarded in some examination systems but at least the assessment of folders of students' writing recommended in the Cox Report (1989) in Great Britain, and teacher assessments of similar kinds of writing elsewhere give some acknowledgement to the potential range of benefits which authentic writing practices can confer upon writers – benefits which can often be of both an intrinsic and extrinsic nature.

The intersubjective and intrasubjective nature of writing

I would like to discuss the intersubjective and intrasubjective nature of writing because it relates closely to my spiral model above. You will recall that the ribs in that model represented various kinds of discourse. Another discourse model which attests to the intersubjective nature of writing is Kinneavy's (1980) concept of writing as involving a Writer, Audience, the Text and the World. This model suggests that at the point of writing writers have to anticipate an audience, draw upon their knowledge of language structures and of the world to create a text which in turn may become part of that world. Although here in Kinneavy's model, and indeed in the function and audience categories of Britton et al. (1975) the intersubjective nature of writing is acknowledged, I think the nature of writing development is best represented as both intersubjective and intrasubjective. That is, writers are influenced by the universe of discourse and they act upon it. I see as central to composing processes the writer's inner world and self-state (self-perceptions and feelings). For example, if I reflect upon the creation of this text, I am aware of searching within my stored experience of readers/audiences, of others' responses to earlier texts I have produced, of my own critical reading eye and of certain affective states influencing my text production, including some anxiety and anticipatory excitement. At this point I have not shared the text with a real reader/audience and something like an integrated focus on thinking and feeling is guiding my production. That is, the process here is intrasubjective, with projected intersubjective engagements with imagined readers influencing me. When a reader/editor makes comments on my text, I will take in those comments and reflect on them in terms of my intended meaning and purpose, possibly changing the text accordingly. That process is both intersubjective and intra-subjective.

At different stages in a writer's development the degree to which the writing process is intrasubjective or intersubjective will vary according to the difficulty of the task and its function. The currently popular conference approach to writing development provides opportunities for writers to have their work responded to in draft form and to internalize a sense of audience responsiveness. However, the approach does need to be carefully planned because not all children know how to respond effectively to others' writing. At some stage both readers and writers need to experience models of effective response in order to know how to respond in turn. The conference approach makes new demands on students as readers and writers and I suspect we currently underestimate what is involved in being a truly constructive and enabling audience/reader.

Writer anxiety

It helps to remind ourselves of the personal investment most committed writers have in their composing processes and products. If authentic writing is a true reflection of self, then writers may feel very vulnerable to public exposure, no matter how apparently democratic or benign the audience or classroom seems to be. As writing development draws upon many internalized linguistic and psycho-logical resources, sensitivity in responding to writers' work in progress is required of readers. In fact, the issue of how we develop students as collaborative readers of each others' writing needs careful planning and sensitivity to classroom dynamics. Teachers who have been involved in extended writing-workshop experiences like those modelled upon the Bay Area approach[2] in the United States, or indeed in any group learning experiences (like drama workshops) involving a measure of self-disclosure will be aware of the need for mutual trust between participants. Such mutual sharing and trust are sometimes in direct contrast to the more common experience of the writing teacher who sets the context for writing but is never actually seen to compose. A real writing teacher, in both senses of the phrase, can be a model and a mentor. If we accept the concept of writing development as an intrasubjective/intersubjective process in which we compose mainly by searching for words, meanings and projections of audiences within our own minds (even if we have had to research a topic by reading and taking notes, or conducting experimental work), having already internalized some models of discourse forms, then it is important for a writing teacher to function as both a writing mentor and positive role model: someone in touch with the realities of writing; someone who values the experience enough to engage in it; someone in whom writers can trust to share their thoughts, feelings and blind spots. Does that description fit most writing teachers?

I hope it is clear now why I am advocating this psychodynamic approach to writing. I see it as providing the essential energizing power for writing. I see it as emphasizing the writer's mind as a dynamic force, able to draw resources for composing from the internalization of experiences, and from the highly individualized interpretations of those experiences, consciously or unconsciously. The interplay between external events and internal states of mind is largely monitored through inner speech. Of course, non-verbalized feelings and the visualization of dreams are also part of the individual's experience of an inter- and intrapsychic world, and they may not come to light through inner speech and writing. None the less, writing can provide a way of focusing, refining and expressing that rich and dynamic interplay so that it is symbolized in words for further reflection and shaping.

Significantly, that is largely the process central to psychoanalysis. In psychoanalysis an analyst acts as the attentive listener and reflecting mirror for the expression of inner speech; in authentic writing, writers monitor their own inner speech, initially. Both psychoanalysis and authentic writing can be processes for the development of the self, though psychoanalysis often functions at a deeper and more conflicted level of unconscious activity than occurs in most writing experiences. None the less, both activities share a potential for shaping and reflecting the self, and both activities are founded on a core belief that most individuals contain within their own psychic structures the means to develop high-order cognitive and emotional integration. Both activities also acknowledge the important influence of the empathic qualities of the significant other. The nature of interpersonal interactions advocated in Heinz Kohut's model of self-psychology has much to offer teachers, just as many teachers will have experiences which can illuminate self-psychology theory.

The practicalities

Given the relatively short time in schools devoted to authentic writing development, each school needs an informed, sustained comprehensive and integrated programme of writing development. This is highly desirable at regional/state level so that primary- and secondary-school teachers can be aware of each others' purposes and objectives. Secondary-school teachers could find inspirational the creative, self-directed, self-initiated writing of which many young writers are capable, under the guidance of informed, attuned teachers of literacy. Here we can witness young children's drive for symbolization through play and language expression, a drive all too often lost as children move up the school grades, possibly because some teachers feel overburdened by accountability and unwittingly try to take over the students' writing and thinking. In so doing they reflect a view of the world which precludes individual exploration of materials and ideas. On the whole, teachers in high schools are less confident than their primary-school colleagues that students will work their way towards desirable patterns of thinking and perceiving if guided rather than driven. It can help if research findings like these and Nancie Atwell's (1987) can provide empirical evidence of the positive personal and public effects of psychodynamic approaches. It also helps if we consider how children learn to speak mainly because they are participants in a language community.

One important feature of that community is the quality of positive encouragement the child receives upon attempting to utter words and phrases. Adults endorse such attempts with enthusiasm, sometimes also modelling the expanded form of the child's utterance. No right-minded adult would prohibit a small child from attempting speech until he/she could utter a complete sentence. The attempt at communication is applauded and the child is endorsed as capable of developing speech. Regrettably the later and arguably more difficult development of writing abilities can be thwarted by adults' inappropriate and premature demands for correctness and the copying of models.

Failure to develop appropriate language abilities

Failure to develop language abilities can also be explained by a psychodynamic theory. The main explanation for such failure, excluding pathological reasons, or physical handicaps such as deafness, would be that the child has had insufficient positive experiences of him/herself as a successful communicator, and insufficient experiences with a range of discourses. It could be that the mirroring audience/reader was not sufficiently empathic to provide appropriate endorsement and enriching language resources for the writer. The degree to which students need such endorsement and resources varies, of course. Some writers are relatively independent quite early, others need mentors, or reflecting audiences, much of their school life. At the formative stages in writing development, writers need empathic reader-audiences who provide appropriate mirroring until they have sufficiently internalized a sense of the multiple audiences they may need to write for. For good readers literature can provide a source of mirroring by implicitly demonstrating various discourse structures. I am thinking of the occasions when we notice a particular usage and think, 'that's a good way of saying it . . . might try something like that myself'.

Also peer audiences provide encouragement and unconscious modelling for writers. It is consistent with a psychodynamic theory of language development to believe that mature writers can imagine or visualize even quite complex, unknown audiences because they have internalized their real or imagined engagements with them.

Obviously, the interplay between speaking, writing, reading, listening, drama and internal reflections is significant in the development of all the language modes. For young children, play, modelling, drawing, dance and all expressive arts can enhance a sense of self as an expressive being.

Certainly it is depressing and alarming for teachers in, say, the later years of high school, to discover students who can barely write a coherent sentence. The temptation is to drill some kind of writing practice which might patch up the problem. Such practices, and the anxiety which can be inherent in the experience for both the teacher and the writer are counter-productive, alienating and rarely successful. I think students need to be encouraged to write about issues, ideas, memories or feelings which matter to them. They need to feel there is a genuine, trusting audience/reader for their expression, and that reader needs to be able to prompt, to read between the lines, to make sense of sometimes incomprehensible language, and to endorse the attempt as far more valuable than its correctness. Only then will writers develop a positive self-concept as a writer, trust the process, read with interest models of various written forms, and persevere with drafting and redrafting. Literacy failure is humiliating, but success can be highly self-affirming. Again, the attitudes and methods implied in these approaches demand time, effort, insight and patience of teachers. None the less, when adults confer with students about their writing, the experience can match, in intention and spirit, the kind of dialogue many adults engage in with very small children as they help them to develop spoken language. Idealization and mirroring can again be significant when students recognize the adult's valuing of them and of writing experiences. It can be an inspiration to self-generated writing, to growth and to an eventual healthy independence of the teacher/audience.

It was interesting to observe how students will persevere with expressive writing even when the activity is physically tiring and the gratification of sharing it with a reader-audience is delayed. If Moffett (1981a) is correct and writing composes the mind, then the process is, presumably, recursive and intrinsically developmental. That is, the writer becomes involved in a self-generated and self-generating process in which the mind and the activity of composing can interplay continuously. The Cox Report (1989) acknowledges this point, rather more simply (14.5).

The spiral model of writing development and the psychodynamic theory informing it arose out of insights gained from the research project outlined in further detail in the following chapters.

The relevance of the theory to classroom practitioners, at all school levels, is that the research informing the theory took account of key factors in writing development: long-term intervention work; writers' capacity to compose, and to internalize, consciously and unconsciously, various audiences and purposes for writing; an attentive adult's need to provide enabling relationships and models of discourse so writers could gain experience and confidence with language.

The psychological factors in language development have been elaborated here to suggest some of the complexities involved in composing written texts. The implications are that such texts provide scope for analysis not just in terms of linguistic structures with which most of us are familiar as English teachers, but in terms of what is revealed about writers' self-concept, self-esteem and self-development. The better able we are to articulate comprehensive writing-development theories, to describe good writing-teaching practices, to understand more deeply the complex dynamics of writing-development processes, the more effective writing teachers we will be.

Summary

- Writers start writing and continue to write because the experience of composing the mind creates its own sense of integration and motivates a continuation of that developmental process. The ensuing self-reflectiveness and reflexiveness of that process does not promote an exclusive egocentricity but expands writers' awareness of their expressive potential, centring them in a much larger universe of discourse.
- Self-reflection and reflexiveness are fundamental to self-development and the personalization of knowledge. Writing can play a part in the development of creative, integrated human beings who can afford to respect the uniqueness of themselves and of others because they have experienced their own capacity to make a mark on the world.
- In the psychodynamic model of writing there is a potential continuity between supposedly different writing functions, such as those termed expressive, poetic and transactional, just as there is between writing for self and writing for others, be they close or distanced.
- Teachers in all curriculum areas have a responsibility to recognize the place of writing in learning and to understand the complexity of writing development; it involves more than an awareness of a variety of audiences and purposes for writing; it involves a complex range of psychological processes which interplay with the cognitive and affective aspects of written symbolization. Teachers can become aware of the potential of authentic writing to compose the mind by engaging in such writing themselves.
- Writers can be influenced by a complex of motivations including a desire to 'see what I mean' through writing, a need to mirror self, to act out aspects of self and to maintain a concept of self as a writer or symbolizer.

Notes

1 The term 'tacit power' or 'tacit abilities' is used here to refer to the intuitive and energizing abilities to develop language which can be released in enabling conditions.
2 The Bay Area Writing Project and the National Writing Project is a network of collaborative school–university programmes to improve writing and the teaching of writing in classrooms in the USA and overseas. It grew out of intensive Summer Institute workshops for teachers at the University of California, Berkeley in the early 1970s and has had an important impact on the writing development of teachers and students in the USA.

3 Assessing writing development

Much of this book is informed by my work in a research project on writing development, particularly in relation to the conclusions below about the assessment of writing.

Briefly, the research project involved a four-year longitudinal study of the development of school children's writing abilities in (school) Years 6 to 9 inclusive. It included an intervention programme of particular writing tasks with experimental students from two Sydney (Australia) primary schools and their subsequent high schools, in order to test an hypothesis that self-expressive, reflective writing tasks would promote students' writing development.

The writing tasks in the intervention programme included exercises in free association, concentration and reflection and a long-term letter-writing exchange between the experimental writers in the two experimental schools.

To assess development in writing, annual writing tests were conducted in the two experimental schools and in four control schools. Assessment of the test writing involved holistic (impression) marking initially, then the development of criteria marking when holistic marking failed to demonstrate development in writing for either the experimental or the control groups over the four-year period. Four criteria were developed – Audience, Creativity, Thinking and Language. The results of the criteria marking provided evidence of significant linear trends in writing development and a significantly higher rate of development in the Thinking category for the experimental group as compared with the control group, but not in the other categories.

A survey of the kinds of writing done across the curriculum over a two-week period in Year 9 in the two experimental high schools showed that a high proportion of the writing done in most subjects, both in school and at home, was note-taking set by the teacher, in contrast to kinds of writing undertaken in the intervention programme.

A major conclusion of the study was that writing development is difficult to detect by purely holistic methods but the application of criteria marking revealed that an intervention programme based on a growth model of writing can achieve some demonstrable effects.

More recently, the four criteria have proved successful in helping teachers in both writing curricula development and the assessment of the effectiveness of writing programmes. The criteria outlines can also be used to provide verbal feedback to writers, helping them to recognize valid aspects of writing and providing some descriptions, or a metalanguage of writing development.

Test writing topics

To illuminate the story of how these four criteria were developed I will outline the annual test writing tasks I devised for my study and comment on the influence upon writers of certain test topics.

I decided that letters would be the appropriate mode of writing for the test writing tasks as they provided a format which is known to most students. As well, letters can provide an encouraging social context for the test tasks, thereby reducing some of the anxiety of a test situation. I also wanted to keep constant one aspect of the test writing tasks (the mode) while increasing the degree of difficulty of the tasks over the four years. It also seemed important not to overcomplicate the task of assessing long-term writing development by unnecessary variation of the writing modes.

Here are the test topics in the form in which they were given to the students each year.

Space (Year 6)
Imagine you have met a friendly visitor from outer space. The visitor came to your school to find out why children write. Could you write him a letter telling him what is easy or hard about writing tasks, why you do them and what makes them enjoyable. Try to help him as much as you can by telling him your ideas and feelings about writing.

Peer (Year 7)
Write a letter to a close friend about any sad, happy or memorable events which have happened to you this year or recently.

Kes (Year 8)
Below is a piece from a novel, Kes, by Barry Hines. The main character in the novel is Billy Casper, a misfit at home and at school. In this part of the story below, Billy has been sent to Mr Gryce's room for falling asleep in assembly. MacDowall has been accused of coughing in assembly and the other three boys were caught smoking.

When you have read the story, imagine you are writing to a pen-friend telling him or her about the boys, Mr Gryce, their behaviour and anything which will help your pen-friend to understand your responses to the story.

Take as long as you need to read the story and to write your letter. Write as much as you like and as freely as you like. [An extract from Kes followed, pages 53–8 of 1979 Penguin edition.]

Principal (Year 9)
Please write as much as you can on the following topic:

Imagine your school principal has asked you what you think about the idea that there should be fewer ordinary lessons in the day and more out-of-class activities such as excursions, concerts, films, sport and drama activities.

Write a letter to the principal outlining your ideas and, most importantly, giving good reasons why your ideas could mean a better education.

(Please note, this letter is for a researcher who is interested in your writing and your ideas. Your letter will not be shown to your principal.)

Future (Year 9)
Imagine you are living in a futuristic age where it is possible to buy a plan for your future life from a 'life-plan agent'.

(The life-plan agent is rather like a travel agent who consults with you about what you want and helps you put together the best plan.)

You like the idea of being able to choose your future life and decide you will go to the life-plan agent. Before you do so WRITE TO A CLOSE FRIEND DISCUSSING WITH HIM/HER WHAT YOU THINK YOU WOULD LIKE THAT PLAN TO BE.

Your plans could include living in other countries or in space, having an interesting career, becoming famous, making a fortune, working to improve conditions on earth, having great adventures or whatever your imagination dreams of.

As you are living in a futuristic age you can be as practical and as imaginative as you like. The friend you are writing to could have some part in your future life or could just be someone to share your ideas with now. (Please sign the letter with your own name.)

Some general comments on the set topics and students' responses

Underlying the composition of the test items was my wish to give every student a chance to make some response to the set topic. As well, I wanted to give scope for the more able writers to perform at their ability level. It is important, I believe, to structure writing topics in such a way that both able and less able students can respond to the best of their ability. If we are seeking, for example, evidence of high levels of thinking ability, then the topic should invite that kind of response in some perceptible way. In composing the content of the *Space* letter I was both interested in students' imaginative responses to the task and their ideas about writing in school. A spaceman was established as the ostensible audience to allow the students to write as 'experts'. The spaceman was the imaginary audience and I was the shadowy audience. As 'experts' with personal experience of school writing, the students could be both helpful and knowledgeable in responding to the spaceman's perceived needs. Although the writers knew that I was the ultimate audience for the writing, they were able to operate effectively with the dual audience, as happens with much school writing anyway. The reflexive and imaginative nature of the task elicited a genuinely communicative response in a very high number of cases. Ninety-two per cent of the writers used the letter-writing format and 78 per cent of writers gave the spaceman an imaginative name (191 scripts were returned for this task). I think the spontaneous naming of the spaceman, apart from the obvious need to address a letter to someone, helped the writers to establish some relationship and empathy with the spaceman. The letters were remarkably engaging and lively, with most writers able to complete the task satisfactorily.

The reasons writers gave for writing in school included comments like 'because the teacher tells you' (15 per cent), 'because it is interesting', 'gives the writer pleasure' (26 per cent), or 'because you learn by writing' (15 per cent). Seventy-nine per cent of writers said they liked writing, and about half of those nominated story writing as a favourite task. I doubt if the students' responses to writing would have been as well differentiated had they been asked simply to list the reasons for writing in school. Context and the style and mode of test topics certainly influence language performance.

The topic *Peer* was chosen because it invited the writers to reflect on personal experience, to write to a peer and to give consideration to their thoughts and feelings. I thought it was broad enough to allow the majority of students to write something. However, I think on reflection it was a fairly mundane topic and I regret not dreaming up something more interesting.

There were several reasons for choosing the extract from *Kes* as the basis of the writing task. I thought that a piece of literature about school life would give the writers something concrete on which to base their letter. The extract could provide an opportunity for students to express their feelings and thoughts about school life, both as portrayed in the extract, and from their own school experiences. As the pseudo pen-friend to whom the letter was addressed presumably did not know the book *Kes*, there was a stated and implicit expectation that the writer could tell enough about the story to put the audience in touch with the context of events.

I also chose the extract from *Kes* because it is an evocative piece about school life, touching upon issues such as smoking, punishment, caning, authoritarianism, injustice, bullying, school routines and the generation gap. It seemed at many levels to invite a range of personal and literary responses to the story. As you might expect at Year 8, few writers actually discussed the literary qualities of the piece, though a few made references to narrative techniques. Those who had the ability to comment on the author's technique and language could do so even in this format.

Most students responded personally and expressively to the task, with considerable variation in ability to decentre and comment on the implications raised by the events in the story. Obviously this task combined with some complexity the skills of reading, listening and writing. The teachers were asked to read the extract aloud as there are some examples of dialect in the piece which could have been difficult for some students. I also edited the extract slightly to shorten it.

On reflection, the choice of an extract from *Kes* was a good one. The piece was fairly long and complex in its implications but it offered several levels of interpretation and some depth of characterization. A number of students expressed interest to their teachers, and in their letters, in reading the book themselves. In all, the choice of the extract fulfilled its purpose in providing a thought-provoking and evocative literary experience as a basis for a letter to a pen-friend. It also elicited a range of responses sufficient to discriminate between writers at this stage of cognitive and emotional development. Apart from the data it provided for comparative purposes in the research, it also provided a range of insights into adolescents' sensitivity (or lack of it) to the ethical issues of justice and punishment.

The letter to the principal was designed to give students an opportunity to reflect on their school experiences and to compose an argument for any changes they might propose. The audience was more distanced than in previous test letters and the writers were expected to be able to consider the notion of a 'better education'.

The *Future* topic was selected for a number of reasons. Because it was the final test piece, I felt it should provide scope for speculative and projective thinking as well as give sufficient stimulus to both able and less able writers. From my observations of the writers in the experimental group, I felt that there were more discernible differences now in the writing and thinking of the able and less able writers in the group. I felt a test topic needed to allow for a range of responses in terms of writers' abilities to handle greater distances in time and space. Hence the requirement that they project into the future and anticipate events by discussing a proposed visit to a life-plan agent with a friend. There was the opportunity for the writers to be tentative, exploratory, familiar, and even ambivalent in working out an imaginary life plan. Within the topic outline, I deliberately suggested alternatives for the writers to consider, covering areas of personal, social and ethical concerns. I felt that my making explicit some abstract considerations, writers could demonstrate a range of responses if they were so inclined and able.

As with all the previous writing tasks, I was the ultimate audience for the writing (as well as the teacher, if he/she chose to read the scripts) but experience with *Space* and *Kes* had demonstrated that students can focus remarkably well on a nominated and imaginary audience if the topic is sufficiently interesting and relevant.

What each writing task required of the writer

Constant factors

The letter-writing format was required for each task. Writers knew that the writing was to be for a researcher from a university.

The timing of the tests (except *Principal*) was constant: the interval after yearly examinations and before end-of-year activities.

As far as possible the instructions to the teachers administering the test were the same each year, except for differences pertaining to the nature of the stimulus; for example, the extract from *Kes* had to be read aloud to the writers.

The teachers were asked to allow the writers a reasonable time to complete the task but there was no long interval of time allowed for writers to revise. Any revision was done within the 'reasonable time' allowed. Usually this time was no longer than two class periods (slightly more for *Kes* where time was allowed for the teacher to read the extract aloud).

Across the five writing tasks there is an increasing degree of difficulty in the cognitive and linguistic abilities needed to complete the tasks effectively. Within the audience category the demands increase only slightly, but within the purposes and intrinsic demands of the five tasks there is a considerable shift with more complex responses needed for *Kes*, *Principal* and *Future*. Finding and demonstrating an appropriate register for writing to the *Principal* proved difficult for some. In each task, except *Future*, the writers were asked to work from known experience. *Kes* was a differently known experience because the writers had to assimilate information given in literary form, select certain personal responses to that information and convey them to the reader with sufficient contextual clues to guide the reader's comprehension. In so doing, the writer has to make complex choices fairly spontaneously, and certainly comprehensively.

The ability to embed information about a story within a responsive and evaluative framework is cognitively and linguistically very demanding. The best writers could be selective, precise, sensitive and perceptive about the complex issues raised in a literature extract. The worst writers could only report that something had happened in the story.

Even this fairly straightforward analysis of the underlying expectations of writers of the test topics demonstrates something of the abilities students need to have developed in order to write well. And I have not even touched on aspects of style, irony, humour, creativity, variability, use of metaphor and the myriad of other features of writing and thinking which influence our creation of meaning.

The influence of topic on writing performance

While research evidence on the influence of writing performance is inconclusive (O'Donnell 1984: 243–9), these test topics do meet a number of the criteria said to identify well-written topics: they did not demand specialized knowledge of subject matter, social conventions or academic conventions; they were clear and explicit so students did not have to read between the lines to determine what was required; they were subjected to critical analysis and rewritten after consultation with colleagues and peer students, and they attempted to provide a balance between open-endedness and directiveness. They had some intrinsic interest and relevance to the writers and they specified an audience beyond the teacher or evaluator.

The matter of selecting good writing topics is one which is an on-going concern as teachers are required to become more accountable for their work. Too often, I suspect, teacher-education courses run out of time to devote to the matter and student teachers probably do not perceive the relevance until they are teaching full time. None the less, part of promoting writing development involves establishing valid and reliable test topics, as well as classroom writing tasks, which alert writers to the vast range of discourse present in literature and life, while enabling them to perceive the implicit and explicit meanings of those discourses.

Writing development involves extremely complex linguistic, cognitive and affective processes and considerable skill is required to compose tests of writing development which are truly valid and, in themselves, developmental. Tests are themselves a very influential part of the language universe.

One of the difficulties I had to face in this study was to determine development over a four-year period. Most test topics are designed to discriminate between students at a similar age/stage period. At the point of developing the test topics I believed that experienced markers could be able to identify growth in writing by holistic marking. In the event, this expectation was not fulfilled so detailed explorations of methods of identifying development of writing abilities had to be undertaken. This involved the development of four criteria for determining growth in writing (see table 3.1).

Development of assessment methods for the test writing tasks

The first criterion I developed was *Audience*. Implicit in the concept of writing development is the notion of writing being addressed to a reader (audience) whom the writer has in mind in the writing process. Of course, some writing like personal diaries and shopping lists may be addressed only to the writer but, as writers develop, the audiences they are increasingly able to address effectively, are potentially more distanced in time and space from themselves. As I have argued earlier here, writers internalize a sense of more distanced audiences as they become more aware of the range of discourse options available, and more sensitive to the potential effects of their writing on readers. Writers' ability to match their awareness of audience with appropriate rhetorical structures depends, of course, on their linguistic and cognitive development or, at least, their tacit development in those areas.

As the ostensible audience for each of the test topics was clearly stipulated in the topic outlines which each writer received, there was not a widely spread level of response in that category over the five topics. Although in each case the writers knew that their test letters were for research purposes, none the less, there was strong evidence that most writers were able to address the audience stipulated in the topic. The only exception to this was a small group of writers from one class who lampooned the *Kes* task and seemed to be writing defensively and self-consciously. (Their responses have led me to further work on the affective and ethical responses of students to the dilemmas raised by the incident in the *Kes* extract.) The degree of audience-awareness evident in the *Space* compositions,

Table 3.1 Criteria for categories of Audience, Creativity, Thinking and Language

(a) AUDIENCE 1–3 (1 is the lowest score)

1	2	3
(a) barely adequate setting of context audience	(a) adequate setting of context	(a) adequate setting of context
(b) some references to audience but simple/low level, e.g. 'Dear Sir'	(b) several references to audience (explicit) e.g. some rhetorical questions, or comments acknowledging or endorsing the audience	(b) several references to audience (explicit)
		(c) several appropriate rhetorical questions OR several instances praising/endorsing audience } metalanguage
		(d) implicit audience awareness in elaboration, details, examples i.e. the writer can balance his/her own concerns with the need to make those concerns interesting to the reader

(b) CREATIVITY 1–5 (1 is the lowest score)

	1	2	3	4	5
EVIDENCE OF CREATIVITY AS:					
ORIGINAL, IMAGINATIVE OR *UNUSUAL IDEAS*	*no evidence*	*some evidence* e.g. – can identify with characters in *Kes* or the spaceman in *Space* – attempt at predictable fantasy	*several instances* but not sustained	*sustained pattern but limited* in scope e.g. humorous – tone of voice – predictable fantasy – well-imagined or re-created story but not *highly* imaginative	*sustained pattern* – broad scope e.g. – speculative/projective thinking – a world view – historic/cultural examples – poetic/metaphoric images – sustained, mature humour – unusual point of view

(c) THINKING 1–6 (1 is the lowest score)

	1	2	3	4	5	6
EXAMPLES GIVEN IN WRITING	– mainly concrete and simple	– concrete and some abstract	– concrete and abstract (narrow range)	– concrete and abstract (narrow range)	– concrete and abstract (broad range: aware of other possibilities)	– concrete and abstract (broad range: aware of other possibilities)
IDEAS	– issues and events seen simplistically	– issues and events seen simplistically	– issues and events seen with some complexity (narrow range)	– issues and events seen with complexity (narrow range)	– issues and events seen with complexity (broad range)	– issues and ideas seen with complexity (broad range)

Table 3.1 *Continued*

POINT OF VIEW						
(a) – egocentric (e.g. what I want should happen)	– mainly egocentric but attempts to see point of view of 'close others'	– can see close others' points of view – 'shades of grey'	– can see close others' and distant others' points of view	– can see close others' and distant others' points of view	– can see close others' and distant others' points of view
(self)	(self and close other)	(self and close other)	(self + close + distant)	(self + close + distant)	(self + close + distant)
(b) – subjective	– subjective mainly	– subjective and objective	– subjective and objective	– subjective and objective	– subjective and objective and 'world view'
METHOD OF PRESENTING POINT OF VIEW in *argument*						
– asserts dogmatically – repetitive	– asserts and gives some supporting evidence – repetitive	– asserts, summarizes, makes relevant, – compares, persuades, some elaboration	– can assert and be tentative – persuades – generalizes – maybe low-level speculate	– asserts/ persuades/can be tentative – structures in hierarchies – elaborates (does not critically evaluate) – maybe low-level speculate (events)	– asserts/ persuades/can be tentative – structures – elaborates/ compares – evaluates (implicitly or explicitly) – speculates from propositions

in *narrative* or *literary response*	– incomplete information and causal links tenuous	– nearly adequate information – causal links just satisfactory	– adequate information and causal links adequate	– information causal links adequate – thematic pattern attempted	– thematic pattern emerging	– thematic pattern established
	– describes states	– describes states	– describes and partly interprets	– describes/ states – interprets	– describes/ states interprets and attempts conclusion reflects	– describes states/reflects/ interprets evaluates concludes (even if not finished) – emphasis implied through structuring
DEGREE OF COMMITMENT TO WRITING TASK	– perfunctory	– some involvement	– seems involved/ committed	– seems involved/ committed	– obviously involved/ committed	– very involved/a belief system emerging
TIME AND SPACE DIMENSION	– barely differentiated (here and now) personal *is* public, fact *is* opinion	– some differentiation (personal and public)	– adequate differentiation (personal and public)	– well differentiated (personal and public) – fact and opinion	– well differentiated	– well differentiated (aware of ambiguities)

Table 3.1 *Continued*

(d) LANGUAGE 1–6 (1 is the lowest score)

	1	2	3	4	5	6
VOCABULARY	– simple	– simple	– simple and abstract	– simple and abstract	– simple and abstract	– simple and abstract
	– maybe imprecise/ inappropriate	– sometimes imprecise/ inappropriate	– precise	– precise – imaginative	– precise – imaginative and poetic	– precise – imaginative/ poetic
	– very few adjectives/ adverbs	– some adjectives/ adverbs	– adjectives/ adverbs	– adjectival/ adverbial clauses	– adjectival/ adverbial clauses and phrases	– adverbial clauses/ phrases
	– often colloquial	– often colloquial	– colloquial and formal/personal and public	– colloquial and formal/personal and public	– colloquial and formal/ personal/ public	– colloquial and formal/ personal/ public
	– very little figurative	– some figurative	– some figurative	– figurative	– figurative/ metaphoric	– figurative and metaphoric
CLAUSES AND SENTENCES Tenses	– mainly present, past, future	– present, past, future	– present, past, generalized present/some conditional	– present/past/ future/general present/ conditional/ passive	– present/past/ future/general present/ conditional/ passive gerunds	– present/past/ future/ conditional/ passive gerunds
	– strung together	– compounded and embedded	– compounded and embedded	– compounded/ embedded/ elaborated	– compounded/ embedded/ elaborated	– compounded/ embedded/ elaborated

	simple cause/effect (illogical/attenuated)	simple cause/effect (some logic)	logical cause/effect	logical cause/effect syllogisms	syllogisms	syllogisms
Cohesion and Register = Coherence (CRC)	– slips	– CRC barely adequate	– CRC almost mastered	– CRC mastered	– CRC mastered	– CRC mastered
Syntax	– rigid	– some flexibility	– flexible	– flexible	– flexible	– flexible
Implicit/explicit	– not clear	– has some idea	– knows	– knows	– knows	– knows
paragraphing/punctuation	– poor/partial	– shaky/partial	– adequate	– adequate	– good	– good
Organization	– poor	– partial	– adequate	– effective	– effective	– focused
Relationship between writing and the experience (purpose)	– barely reported	– reported	– partly general	– clearly general	– explored/analysed/synthesized	– explored/analysed/synthesized/evaluated (even implicitly)
Rhetorical sophistication	– none	– very little	– some	– discernible/some humour	– clearly apparent and humour	– clearly apparent humour and irony and satire and ambiguity
Style (individual voice)	– none	– very little	– some	– emerging pattern	– well developed	– well developed

even when the audience was ostensibly an imaginary spaceman, was substantial. It may be that imaginary audiences are particularly enticing.

Although the ability to anticipate and meet the needs of a reader/audience is reflected in a writer's cognitive strategies and linguistic structures in writing, and separate categories were devised for those abilities, I considered that audience awareness as a significant feature of writing development merited a separate category.

Marking according to categories or criteria was designed essentially as a way of assisting markers to focus on the distinguishable and relevant features of writing which help determine development in writing.

I will now outline below the four criteria developed to determine long-term development (see Appendix A for the outlines of the criteria).

Audience category

This category has a three-point scale with 1 as the lowest point.

A composition scoring 1 in this category would have a barely adequate setting of context for the audience. There may be some explicit references to the audience but these would be simple, for example, 'Dear Sir', or 'Yours truly'. Writers scoring 1 would demonstrate little more than conventional awareness of their audience.

A composition scoring 2 would demonstrate an adequate setting of context. For example, in *Space* reference might be made to the fact that writing was an important part of school life, or in *Kes* some references might be made to events in the story. There could also be some references to the audience in the body of the letter, for example, rhetorical questions posed or some explicit phrases which endorse or acknowledge the audience.

A composition scoring 3 would demonstrate a very clear awareness of audience. This would be evident in an adequate setting of context. There may be several explicit references to the audience and implicit audience-awareness demonstrated in appropriate elaboration and in the choice of details and examples given in the letter. Writers scoring 3 for *Audience* would demonstrate the ability to balance their own concerns with the need to make those concerns interesting to the reader/audience. This is an ability to entice and hold the reader's interest.

Language category

The second criterion developed was *Language*. Language refers to the linguistic features evident in the composition. Drawing on the evidence of the compositions in the core sample, I made choices about the kinds of linguistic features I believed reflected development in written language ability. I used the broad vertical headings of *Vocabulary*, *Clauses and Sentences* and *Structuring* with subsets across a six-point scale on which were listed the linguistic features likely to be found on each point on the scale.

Under the heading of *Vocabulary*, for example, a composition scoring 1 would have simple vocabulary which may be imprecise or inappropriate; there would be few adjectives or adverbs, and very little figurative language. By contrast, a composition scoring 6 might have a range of vocabulary: simple and abstract; precise; imaginative/poetic; colloquial and formal, figurative and metaphoric. Overall, the writer would create the impression that he/she had a command of vocabulary, even though not all features listed under a score of 6 were demonstrated.

Under the heading of *Clauses and Sentences*, a composition scoring 2, for example, might show the use of present, past and future tenses, compounded and embedded sentences and some simple cause/effect relationships. A composition scoring 5 for *Language* might show the use of present, past and future tenses but also the conditional tense, passive voice and gerunds. There could be compounded, embedded and elaborated clauses and sentences. There might also be evidence of some syllogisms, demonstrating the writer's more complex awareness of cause/effect relationships than that of a writer scoring 2 on this scale.

Under the heading *Structuring*, there were several subheadings including cohesion and register (which together demonstrate coherence), syntax, organization, rhetorical sophistication and style. Obviously the marker has to make a holistic judgement of the writer's language development, taking into account the presence or absence of these features and awarding the score appropriate to the best fitting description of the writer's language.

A composition scoring 3 on the *Language* scale might demonstrate in its structuring that cohesion and register are almost mastered, that syntax is flexible and that the writer knows when to be explicit and when to be implicit. Paragraphing and punctuation would be adequate; there would be some rhetorical sophistication, as in word play or asides, and some sense of the writer's style.

A composition scoring 6 on the *Language* scale would show mastery of all the features listed under *Structuring* and there may be some implicit or explicit evaluation of the experience being written about. For example, in writing the letter to the principal (*Principal*) about ways to improve school life, writers scoring 6 might question their own statements about existing educational practices. Humour, irony, satire and awareness of ambiguity in one's own ideas or others' might be demonstrated.

A composition scoring 6 would give a clear sense of the writer's individual voice and style as well as demonstrable ability in a broad and complex range of language options.

As with all the categories devised for the markers' guidance, the purpose was to list and to calibrate those features of the category most likely to appear in a composition to be awarded each point on the scale. Markers still had to make a summary judgement for each of the four criteria, guided by the features listed in the scale. If a marker was unsure of the appropriate scale, it could help if a judgement were made based on a best-fitting description; then the descriptions on adjoining scales were read to determine the wisdom of the original choice.

In developing the *Language* scale I was influenced by the range of features evident in the compositions from *Space* to *Future* and by the developmental trends in language use postulated by Moffett and Wagner in their *Student-Centered Language Arts and Reading K-13* (1976). The broad theoretical assumption underlying the development in these criteria is that written-language development is reflected in the writer's ability to use with increased effectiveness a whole range of discourse options according to the desired function or purpose of the writing.

Thinking category

The third criterion developed was the *Thinking* category. Again I developed a six-point scale for this category to account for the range of cognitive structures relevant to written discourse and evident in the compositions in the core sample. The subheadings in the *Thinking* category related to features such as the range of ideas in the writing, the presentation of the writer's story or argument, the ability to see others' points of view and the writer's ability to differentiate in the time and space dimension.

The broad theoretical basis for this category was the belief that with increasing maturity writers are able to think both simply and complexly and to see the world from both a personal and objective, or decentred point of view. The notion of seeing the world from a decentred point of view refers to the ability to take account of others' points of view, even in an imaginative or projected way, and to the ability to distinguish between self and others, between fact and opinion and between thought and feeling. It also includes the ability to think beyond the immediate and to project into the future in speculative propositions.

A composition scoring 2 in the *Thinking* category would give mainly concrete examples and present ideas simplistically. The writer's point of view would be mainly egocentric with some attempt made to see the points of view of close others. In presenting an argument the writers would make assertions and give some supporting evidence but the points of view presented could be repetitive rather than developed. In narrative or literary response, a writer scoring 2 would give just enough information for the reader to be able to identify the context. In the time and space dimension, the writer would show some ability to differentiate between personal and public points of view and there would be some sense of his/her ability to think beyond the immediate and present.

By contrast, a writer scoring 4 on the *Thinking* category would be able to see both close others' and distant others' points of view. Ideas would be presented with some complexity and the writer would be able to persuade, generalize and, maybe, speculate at a low level. The speculation might concern an idea close to the writer's concerns rather than an issue of world importance. There would be a sense of commitment and involvement in the writing and evidence of the writer's ability to differentiate between personal and public concerns and to distinguish between fact and opinion. There could be some thematic pattern, in embryonic form, emerging in the composition.

Creativity category

The fourth and final category I developed was *Creativity*. Essentially, creativity as a criterion of writing development relates to the original, imaginative or unusual ideas presented in the writing. Although creativity is rarely used as a separate criterion in assessing writing development, I thought that after reading and assessing the compositions for the other three criteria, there was still a feature of writing evident in some compositions which had not been accounted for in the existing criteria. Some account had been given of creativity in language within the vocabulary and structuring subsets of the *Language* category, but sustained creativity of ideas had not, so far, been rewarded.

Again, by reading the compositions in the core sample, focusing on creativity of ideas, I developed a scale of five points this time. The only subheading in the creativity category was original, imaginative or unusual ideas. A composition scoring 1 on this scale would show some evidence of such ideas. To score 3 on this scale, the writer would give several instances of original, imaginative or unusual ideas but those ideas would not be sustained or elaborated in any detail. To score 4 on the scale, a writer would have a sustained pattern of original, imaginative or unusual ideas, but that pattern, though sustained throughout the writing, would be limited in scope. For example, the writer might sustain a humorous or ironic of voice in the composition but there would be little else in the composition which showed creativity as defined here. A composition scoring five would have a sustained pattern of imaginative ideas and within that pattern there would be a broad scope of imaginative ideas. For example, such a writer might demonstrate an ironic tone of voice (sustained pattern) as well as poetic or metaphoric images to support, for example, an argument. Likewise, historical and cultural examples might be cited to support some radical ideas about changes in the education system, for example. While creativity of ideas relates to cognitive and linguistic processes, it merited a separate category to ensure that adequate attention was given in the assessment procedures to significant features of writing development.

In essence, the development of these criteria was an attempt to guide markers in their task of perceiving and rewarding those aspects of written discourse which together (or even separately) mark a writer's movement towards maturity in writing. Although the categories interrelate, and obviously the markers are reading the same whole texts each time they mark for the distinctive categories, the merit of this approach to detecting development seems to be that it helps readers/markers to focus on the evidence before them rather than on some preconceived norm or some implicit and possibly irrelevant category.

I did consider whether I needed a *Purpose* category which would have focused on how well the writer fulfilled the demands of the letter-writing tasks. I decided that the features of writing relevant to that purpose were already accounted for in the existing four categories.

I also considered the need for an *Affective* or *Feeling* category and again decided that the existing categories gave adequate account for the relevant features of writing present in the core sample. None the less, I think there is a case to be made for writing to be analysed in terms of the writer's awareness of feelings, and scope for developing through writing one's increased ability to differentiate feeling.

The main purpose for developing categories suitable for this study was to provide sufficient guidelines for markers to be able to detect growth in writing over and above the influence of topic variation. It is not assumed that these criteria alone account for all development in writing; rather, they provide a sufficiently comprehensive, valid and reliable measure of the features most likely to reflect maturity over a long period of time.

Once I had completed the criteria categories, I marked all 195 compositions in the core sample on all criteria. I read and marked the compositions in sets of five topics in the randomized order used for holistic marking.

Marking in categories by single experienced marker

The experienced marker previously involved in holistic marking of the core sample was briefed on the revised assessment procedures so she could mark the core sample according to the criteria and provide scores to correlate my marks with hers. We found that the categories were identifiable to both of us with a high level of agreement *and* that, based on the four criteria, development in writing ability could be discerned.

The main purpose of my study (see Appendix A) was to test the effectiveness of a longitudinal writing programme in terms of the language and thinking abilities of the experimental students in comparison with their peers in the control group. The experimental students were encouraged to write expressively and personally, with a view to their becoming increasingly able to use language more appropriately and flexibly and to think with increased differentiation. The only one of the four categories in which the experimental group developed their writing more than the control group was in that of *Thinking*.

Possible reasons for the differential increase in the Thinking category

In essence, the writing activities of the experimental students involved, initially, experiences in writing spontaneously and in relatively unstructured ways in order to gain confidence in writing, and to recognize the initial source and audience for writing as within one's self. As I said earlier, at the start of the writing programme, the students wrote free-association pieces and personal reflections on significant events. At that stage I was the only audience for the writing. Gradually, the students reached a stage where they wanted to make their writing available to others and on their initiative the letter-writing exchange was set up. The fact that the writers sought audiences other than themselves suggests, I think, that, when writers are sufficiently in tune with and comfortable about their own writing and thinking, they will often seek to share it with others. It seems that once an internal monologue shifts to become a written dialogue (even with self as the primary audience) and the writing process has served the writer's own internal purposes, the overtly social nature of language asserts its influence. The writing can be shared.

The timing of the movement from writing where the self is the sole audience to writing where the self is one-among-many audiences varies for individuals and for different written modes. In this writing programme there was an apparently natural progression in audience from self-as-primary audience to close others as audiences, when sufficient time had been allowed for writers to find themselves in their own relatively spontaneous writing. Sometimes, it seems, to discover oneself in writing (or in other symbolic/communicative acts) motivates a need to communicate with others and to disclose oneself in some part.

Comments made in the early spontaneous writing done by students where they were asked to continue recording their thoughts ('I am thinking about . . .') reveal the potential for self-discovery in expressive, personal writing: 'That is the first time I knew what I thought.' The ability to differentiate thought and to recognize others' points of view, depends, arguably, on being self-aware. Judging by the students' responses and their wish to write to their peers, writing contexts which encourage a continuing relationship both with the self and between self and others can enhance awareness of selves as individuals and selves in relationship with others. The test results suggest that this can lead to development in decentring and thinking ability.

The letter-writing exchange which formed the greatest part of the intervention writing programme, allowed the writing partners to be collaborators in writing, and also, implicitly, evaluators of each others' writing. The positive effect of the relationships established through the letter writing was that writing partners, after the initial exploratory stages of the relationship, could take some risks with their writing. They could even make mistakes in the degree of explicitness or inexplicitness in their language, knowing that obscurities in meaning could be signalled by their partner.

Unlike most regular school writing, the letter exchange was a continuing process which allowed scope for the normal ebb and flow of relationships and learning. As well, many writers had a sense of ownership with their own and their partner's writing, recognizing the responsibilities of reciprocity and mutuality. This is illustrated in the case study of Anna and Jane later on. Even poor writers who had difficulty elaborating the content of their letters rarely failed to meet the social conventions of tact and sensitivity in acknowledging the efforts of their often more able writing partner. Even where there were obvious mismatches in the relative abilities of the writing partners, there was a strong motivation to continue the writing relationship, as if the self-endorsing quality of the experience had its own reward.

A further insight into reasons for the effectiveness of the writing programme in terms of thinking development, is offered in Hillocks' (1986) discussion of the role of declarative knowledge and procedural knowledge in discourse development. Declarative knowledge allows for the identification of phenomena and for the naming and recall of information stored in memory. By contrast, procedural knowledge involves the ability to produce, transform or substantiate that knowledge. Citing the work of Bereiter and Scardamalia (1982) on the influence of procedural knowledge on the conduct of memory searches, even without the prompting of a conversational partner, Hillocks' (1986) analysis of the potential applicability of these theoretical distinctions between knowing what and knowing how also adds some substance to the reasons offered here for the role of the letter exchange in developing students' thinking. For example, two writing partners, Juliet and Simon, demonstrated the role of declarative knowledge and of procedural knowledge in the development of their own letter-writing strategies. Juliet chose to write one of her early letters to Simon partly in point form. After the conventional letter opening, she wrote the rest of her comments and information in twenty-two points; some more elaborated than others. In his reply, Simon also wrote twenty-two points but commented, 'I think your last letter was too long. Please do not write so much.' He knew how to write a letter (albeit point form for a letter is not strictly conventional), and attempted to match Juliet's achievement. Simon was able to use effectively the model provided by his writing partner, notwithstanding the effort involved in matching her, a timely reminder of the powerful influence of adult and peer modelling in child language development. The wish to be part of a language community and to match its models of discourse is particularly influential within rewarding and endorsing relationships.

Hillocks also refers to Bereiter and Scardamalia's (1982) work on schemas for writing where they argue for the need for conversational partners to initiate memory searches. The conversational partners help each other to call up information. Clearly the letter exchange provided the writers with a conversational partner, albeit one with whom the conversation was conducted through letters. In spite of the inevitable delay between the exchange of letters, the conversational nature of such letters and the reciprocity between the partners possibly assisted the memory searches which Bereiter and Scardamalia speculate (Hillocks 1986: 76) are a starting point in writing development.

It is worth recalling here also that some of the experimental writers continued with both their exchange letters and their personal writing such as journals and stories. This happened most commonly where there was a mismatch in abilities between the partners (see Tanya's case study, page 59). Undoubtedly some writers more than others can use more effectively and flexibly the range of resources available in the environment. Where two writing partners were particularly well matched, as were Jane and Anna (see case study, page 80), they shared stories and poems as well as letters and sought each other's comments on their writing.

Although several writing partners wished to help each other with writing, where one partner was a better writer than the other, the help was usually in terms of providing implicit models for writing, or in terms of providing unqualified support rather than specific advice.

For all that the letter exchange provided in terms of positive reinforcement and modelling of language structures, it failed to provide the kinds of analytic and specific help which an adult/teacher might offer. Clearly the time comes when a supportive relationship alone cannot provide the full range of experiences and resources needed for writing development. Some writers in the programme recognized this themselves and sought specific help from me. It would have been interesting to have extended the letter exchange and had writing partners comment specifically on each other's work. Done sensitively, perhaps modelled on a good teacher's methods of responding to writing, it could be an effective form of peer conferencing through writing.

The role of mirroring between the writing partners could also account for the positive effect of the intervention programme on the students' thinking abilities. The mirroring process is evident in the example given above of Juliet and Simon. When there is mutuality in a relationship, or the desire for it, there is often an unconscious mirroring process involved. That is, the partners strive to achieve a balance in the dynamics of their relationship such that each partner can feel comfortable about their similarities and differences. As mentioned earlier, analyses of the early letters showed a high level of self-esteem comments exchanged by the students. Without fail, all students used some self-esteem comments in their early letters. It seems they had a tacit understanding of how to establish a positive relationship, presumably because they had some awareness of how they like to be responded to themselves. It is doubtful whether even the best teachers could engage in the kinds of exchanges with students which the peer-letter writing allowed, because of the established power relationships between students and teachers. Rather like the students' identification with the concerns of the imaginary spaceman in the first test letter, students in the letter-writing exchange felt in touch with the concerns of their peers simply through the commonality of age and experience. They expected to understand each others' language and implicitly mirrored mutual regard and a positive valuing of writing through their letters. In the dynamics of the writing process these aspects are largely unconscious in the writers. Attitudes and feelings gained from a multitude of prior language experiences are transferred unconsciously to the new experience. What might have also helped this peer-teaching experience was the unqualified optimism of the students. They had no store of negative experiences from a peer-letter exchange, though, as you will see in the case study of Jane and Anna, that is not to say such an exchange was conflict free. The special quality in the conflicts encountered by Jane and Anna was the positive working-through, or resolution, of those conflicts through the exchange of letters, a rare quality in student–teacher conflicts. Anna told me several years after the study finished that she remembered feeling excited about the prospect of a pen-friend who had no prior knowledge of her, someone who would not know or care whether she was part of the 'in' group at school or not.

In summary, the positive influence of the writing-intervention programme on students' thinking abilities was probably due to a number of factors; the progression from writing spontaneously for self to writing in more considered ways to a peer-partner; the release of tacit powers of decentring through the experience of becoming more self-aware and concomitantly more other-aware, and the unconscious effects of mirroring, modelling and positive relating abilities in the dynamics of the letter-writing exchange.

Possible reasons for lack of significant development in other categories

There are a number of plausible reasons why there was a lack of significant development in the audience, language and creativity abilities of the experimental writers over the control writers.

This writing intervention programme was different in its focus and emphases to the kinds of writing being done in the regular schools' programmes. A survey of the kinds of writing done in a two-week period in the Year 9 classes in the experimental schools demonstrated that the writing activities in the intervention-writing programme were distinctly different to those done in regular classes and that the major kind of school writing across the curriculum in Year 9 was transactional writing or note-taking.

Whatever the complex reasons for the apparent failure of policies of language across the curriculum to be effectively implemented in most schools in this country, it is clear that the effectiveness of imaginative and expressive writing practices needs to be more convincingly argued and demonstrated, especially for secondary schools. As well, the connections between different kinds of writing need to be elaborated and understood so there is a smooth transition between expressive writing and transactional writing as a product of a well-integrated school writing programme. It is not sufficient to provide isolated writing experiences, however well intentioned and theoretically defensible, unless there is consistency and reinforcement provided within the larger school environment, and indeed education bureaucracies. This kind of study might have been more effective as a school-based team project involving teachers across the curriculum with an enthusiasm for writing development.

It is also clear from this study that not only is development in writing slow to occur, but where it does occur at all it is also difficult to detect. In an effective developmental writing programme the process and progress of such a programme need to be constantly reviewed and revised while it is operating, preferably guided by appropriate developmental criteria. I wish I had had at the beginning of the study the criteria outlines I developed after the intervention programme finished.

In view of the demonstrable lack of reinforcement of expressive writing in the students' regular lessons, my fortnightly visits to the schools were inadequate to create the complexity of changes I was hoping for. While it is easy to blame lack of time for a particular result, I do think there is generally a lack of awareness of the amount of time and practice needed to develop the complex skills of writing effectively. At times I look with envy at the enthusiasm and time given to sports practice! And at the rewards and esteem given to sporting achievements.

In my work in the schools, I experienced the same frustrations as class-teachers dealing with cancelled school periods, absenteeism, examinations and various interruptions to routine. The continued goodwill of the participating schools and the writers was encouraging, but goodwill alone does not create effectiveness; writing development needs sustained writing practice and more time devoted to it than is now the case. A step in the right direction would be for two hours per day to be devoted to integrated language practice. As well, an effective writing programme needs to provide appropriate modifications to cater for the spread of writing abilities across even the same grade. Surprisingly, most of the writers, even the poorer ones, maintained interest in the writing pro-gramme over the four-year period; this suggests it had some intrinsic interest for them. The experimental writers in this study provided a comprehensive range of abilities from the barely articulate to the rhetorically sophisticated. Providing enrichment and variety for that range of abilities is challenging even for one with an avowed interest in writing development.

Overall, one of the reasons for the lack of significant development in the *Language, Creativity* and *Audience* categories then was the lack of intensive, consistent time available in once-fortnightly sessions without reinforcement in regular classes.

Although I thought there might be significant development in the *Audience* category for the experimental group compared with the control group, I think I can now see why that did not occur. *Audience* was the least discriminatory category and the lack of significant development at least showed that the experimental group were not advantaged by the topics' requirement that they write mainly to a peer audience, as they had been doing in the exchange letters. It is interesting that the significant difference showed up in the *Thinking* category which was more finely tuned than the *Audience* category. It suggests that the experience of the letter exchange had developed the experimental writers' ability to see the world and others in more finely differentiated ways as a result of identifying with the needs and responses of a peer audience.

You will recall that the *Creativity* category was devised primarily to reward those writers who demonstrated original, unusual or imaginative ideas even where their thought and language might not have done justice to those ideas. (There was provision for creativity in language within the *Language* category.) Given the arguable emphasis on convergent thinking in most school practices, and the emphasis on transmission methods of teaching and learning, it is not surprising that there was little evidence of divergent thinking among either the control group writers or the experimental writers. While the intervention writing programme provided encouragement for the demonstration of original and imaginative ideas in the free-association and spontaneous writing, and in the test writing topics, it may be that some of those students who are capable of creative thought are not sufficiently confident of its value to adults/examiners to demonstrate it in test writing. If ever there is a time to get things right by adults' expectations, it is in tests. Among the able writers like Anna, Tanya and Jane (see case studies) there is evidence of creative thought in both their test writing and their intervention-programme writing, but the marginally able writers like Anton and Simon (see case studies) who frequently showed creative thought in their non-test writing, took no risks in their test writing and kept to fairly formulaic approaches. The same argument could apply to many writers who 'play safe' for all kinds of reasons in test and non-test situations. There was no particular emphasis in the intervention programme on the sustained development of creative ideas, though such an emphasis could be well justified.

It may be that writers themselves, and their teachers, need more clarification on what constitutes development in writing. I wish I could start my study all over again, knowing what I know now! It is clear that those students who are concerned about their development in school take pains to guess what teachers/examiners reward. In this study, some experimental writers in Year 6 talked to me about their perceived expectations of teachers in secondary school, in anticipation of meeting those expectations. Arguably, if such students could perceive, discuss, experiment with and internalize the defensible criteria of writing development, such declarative knowledge might translate into procedural knowledge. That is, the covert might become overt and operable.

With hindsight, a more open and detailed exploration with the experimental writers of what constitutes writing development might have improved the students' writing and the effectiveness of this study.

As peer interaction can be influential in promoting some kinds of development, particularly thinking abilities, clearer insight into those aspects of writing development which can be enhanced by such interaction, and those aspects which need teacher direction could more fruitfully utilize the potential of the classroom environment. It appears that positive relationships between peers and between students and teachers provide stimulus to certain kinds of thinking, but the further elaboration or differentiation of such thinking (and creativity and language) might need the analysis and evaluative responses of adult or sophisticated respondents to writing. That is, studies in writing research may need to provide clearer differentiation of those aspects of development which are best promoted in particular contexts. Although there was some measure of correlation between the four categories used to measure development in this study, there was also sufficient discrimination between the categories to merit focusing on them separately in an integrated writing programme. Because writing development requires a complex of thinking, feeling and linguistic responses within differing social and political contexts, even when writers have developed the means to demonstrate their rhetorical sophistication, they need to exercise sound judgement and insight in making appropriate choices from their repertoire. Writers in secondary school need to understand in a finely differentiated way what constitutes good writing. Extensive practice in authentic writing and wide reading will help that understanding. Peer audiences have an important part to play in writing development, as do wider audiences, various models of writing and effective writing teachers.

The reading and analysing of effective pieces of writing in various modes are traditional comprehension practices in many senior English classes, but it is less common for such writing to provide models for student writing. What I have in mind is not the slavish imitation of another's language, but the opportunity for comparisons to be made between, say, established authors writing on a topic which students might also write about. If the models are historical pieces, comparisons can be made on all kinds of differences between usage then and now.

In essence, what I am arguing for is a closer concentration on helping students to understand some of the complexities of writing effectiveness. In my study the intervention programme made a significant difference to the writers' ability to take into account the needs and expectations of others in their own composing processes. This happened without specific planning but was a developmental response to the contexts of the letter exchange which was then generalized to the students' test writing. The criteria I developed for assessment purposes do provide guidelines for writing curriculum because they specify discourse features which we can reasonably expect to find in the writing of secondary-school students. They are not so specific in detail that they apply only to the letter-writing mode: teachers have used them effectively for a number of different kinds of writing. If certain contexts do promote certain aspects of writing development, then we need to think carefully about the writing practices which best provide a range of contexts conducive to the development of audience abilities, language abilities, creativity and thinking. Again, as writing teachers we cannot do it all alone; we need to engage our students' tacit abilities and their abilities to integrate, and generalize from a range of personally meaningful experiences.

Summary

- We need to give considerable attention to the composition of test essay topics so that most students at the relevant age and stage are able to respond.
- If the purpose of the test is to determine particular linguistic or cognitive abilities in students, then the test topic must invite the required response, either by the stipulation of a particular audience, or by the requirement that the writer demonstrates ability to vary language and cope with various dimensions of time or space. The fear is unfounded that a well-articulated test

topic with clear expectations might mean that insufficient discrimination will occur between writers.

- A method of 'holistic-criteria' marking such as eventually used here can be more successful in providing evidence of long-term development than simple holistic or impression marking.
- The criteria outlines can be applied to a range of writing modes and across a fairly wide age/stage range. Modifications can be made where appropriate. They can apply to reading development and oral development as well.
- The most plausible reason for the significant improvement in the Thinking category for the experimental students over the control students is the effect of peer writing in promoting students' ability to decentre, and to take into account the needs and expectations of others. The lack of significant improvement in the Audience, Language and Creativity categories highlights the need for more intensive writing practice in schools and greater understanding of the complex nature of writing development.

4 Tanya: an outstanding writer

Since time immemorial we have told stories to illuminate a point of view. I hope the stories I tell in the following case studies provide interesting insights into the minds and processes of writers, while adding colour and depth to the empirical research findings reported earlier. My work with the intervention writers strongly influenced my development of the psychodynamic spiral theory outlined in chapter 3 so these stories may reveal the source of some of that influence. Such is the nature of reading that you will make connections that I have missed and reach conclusions relevant to your own view of teaching and learning. So it should be.

I have selected these particular writers for varying reasons. They can all tell us something about the motivations, difficulties, strategies, thoughts and feelings involved in the process of writing. They all help us to see the idiosyncrasies of writing processes and the sensitive awareness necessary for effective literacy teaching. Narratives can often help us make sense of numbers and theories.

The general framework for the analysis of the case-study writers' work will be the four criteria, Audience, Creativity, Thinking and Language, together with generalizations about their approaches to writing and their apparent psychological processes.

I chose these particular case-study writers to provide a balanced and representative picture of outstanding writers, middle-range writers and poor writers. Because there were more girls than boys in the experimental group, the need to provide a range of writing abilities has taken precedence over a male–female ratio.

An outstanding writer – Tanya

Tanya was a student in the all-girls experimental school and she was merited close attention here for a number of reasons: she presented as a student with a particular interest in writing and in her own thought processes; she responded very quickly to my offer to be an 'interested adult audience' for her writing, and she was imaginative, mature and intelligent. She was an able writer with enthusiastic responsiveness to adult attention and encouragement. Although she was likely to blame herself if such support were not forthcoming, she was ready to gain from and give to an enabling environment.

In the intervention writing programme, Tanya wrote nineteen letters to Lino, her writing partner, nine narrative or reflective pieces, many journal entries and several poems. Three structured letters were written as an exercise in adopting different points of view: a reply to an advertisement for a country holiday with a host family, a letter supposedly written while on that holiday and a thank-you letter after the imagined experience. In Tanya's journal or diary she often expressed her ideas and feelings as precursors to more extended letters or stories. As far as possible here I will present Tanya's writing history chronologically.

When I first met Tanya in Year 6 she was quite forthcoming about her attitudes to writing, including her preference for writing in class instead of listening to the teacher. She liked to believe there was an interested reader for her writing, even in the absence of such a reality. As you will see, she had the ability to seek and to use effectively the resources available around her for the process and development of writing. These resources included adults, peers, literature, cultural experiences and life itself. She thought her ideas became better when she wrote in different ways and she seemed to have a tacit awareness of the value of writing in learning.

In Year 6 Tanya's teacher was an imaginative woman who encouraged the students to write stories in their English classes, though much of their note-making in other subjects was a traditional summary of the text-book.

In the second interview I had with Tanya I discussed the purpose of the research study and my interest in writing development. In response Tanya offered the following observations about writing in school, implicitly revealing her expectations of the secondary school into which she would move the following year:

> *Tanya*:   You want to see how my writing develops . . . well, as you get older . . . when you're little your ideas are really babyish . . . you've got more imagination so ideas tend to be crazy. When you get older and write stories it changes a lot because you don't make it so imaginative.
>
> *Author*:   Do you think that's a pity?
>
> *Tanya*:   Sometimes little children's stories seem funny. (They) seem more real when you are older.

In the first interview I had encouraged Tanya to start writing a journal. I now asked her if she had made any discoveries about writing as she was writing her journal. She replied: 'It made me feel better . . . (I) sort of write down what I felt, can't keep a diary, I forget.'

Tanya saw the journal as different to a diary because she would discuss the journal with me. She really did value the sense of an interested reader. When I asked her if her journal writing was any different to the writing she did in school, she replied: 'In history projects it's facts about a famous person that's about yourself [the journal] and how you feel . . . In history projects I copy from the book, word for word, or ideas that are important.'

In the third interview I asked Tanya more about the kinds of writing she did at school. Apart from stories, Tanya perceived her writing in natural science, history, geography, general studies, English (sometimes) and reading as 'factual'. She had enjoyed doing a writing task which I had set to be written in a normal English class under the teacher's direction: 'My ideal school.' She said of that piece: 'It made me feel better . . . you were writing what you felt the school would be like . . . you forgot dreary old school . . . you felt better.'

I asked who she was writing the piece for: 'For my friends and myself . . . If we could do it (have an ideal school) it would be really good . . . you could write what we thought . . . nobody could contradict what we thought . . . own opinion.'

In her Ideal School piece Tanya wrote about having a school, located in the Sahara Desert beside an oasis . . .

> After lessons we would swim in the shallow parts of the oasis for one hour and then two hours of silent reading . . . The good part about my school would be that the children would be more willing to learn things because the lessons would be fun and the facts wouldn't be shoved down your throat like they are at normal schools.

(The class teacher wrote at the bottom of this, 'I hope not.')

Clearly Tanya was feeling some conflict between the perceived demands of school work to be factual and concrete, and her own interest and pleasure in reflective and imaginative work. To some extent that conflict persisted throughout the period of the research study and I became increasingly relied upon as an adult who positively encouraged Tanya to develop both the cognitive and affective aspects of her very active mind.

In the third interview I asked Tanya more about the journal she had started earlier but had stopped writing over the period of the August vacation.

Tanya: I feel better that I'm writing down things that happened instead of keeping them shut up.

Author: Why did you stop [writing the journal]?

Tanya: Couldn't be bothered . . . was going out over the holidays.

Author: What would help keep it going?

Tanya: Better if doing it just for self . . . personal things.

Author: Are there differences in writing for different people?

Tanya: If writing for yourself make more of an effort. For the teacher it's the same you do everyday . . . you don't have any feeling for it . . . when you do it for yourself it makes it more interesting, don't feel so bored . . . don't feel so dull.

Author: Do you know the kind of pattern the teacher would approve of?

Tanya: Yes, sort of . . . in a project I do it word for word. [She then expressed renewed interest in writing for herself again in the journal.] It's much better really.

In the same interview Tanya spoke about her new interest in becoming an astronomer, a change from her wish to become a geologist. She was interested now in black holes and the sun:

> *Tanya*: Nowadays everybody thinks I'm mad . . . a student teacher didn't think I was smart enough to do it [become an astronomer]. If facts are interesting I want to tell everyone about it.
> *Author*: Perhaps you could write those interesting things in a story.

The sequel to that last comment was that, two months later, Tanya wrote a novel, *The Twelve Tasks*, a science fiction story complete with chapters and an effective plot, galactic adventures and accurate references to 'gravitational pull' and lasers. She dedicated the novel to me.

Up to this point my involvement with Tanya had been limited to four interviews where, in part, I had expressed interest in Tanya as a writer of both factual and imaginative pieces. It is possible that I provided some symbolic resolution of the conflict Tanya was having about practising and experimenting with different kinds of writing. Tanya seemed relieved to have found a mentor for her writing.

The novel Tanya wrote is too long to quote in full but its structure, use of narrative generalization, dialogue, characterization and imaginatively sustained setting, together with its carefully lettered headings, illustrative photos and map, mark the work as a most accomplished piece of fiction for a Year 6 student at the end of her primary schooling.

Tanya developed very quickly a strong image of me as an interested adult reader for her writing. It is quite humbling and even intimidating to realize how influential we can be! After she had written her letter to a spaceman (*Space*), she told me 'I knew you'd read it so I was doing it knowing that . . . so not as I'd do it to [another person] . . . if really a spaceman I'd have to do it so he'd really understand.'

Tanya had correctly assumed that I was the real audience for the spaceman letter and she was able to balance the demands of that real audience with those of the imaginary audience, the spaceman. In itself this ability is not remarkable but it does remind us of one of the many complexities students have to deal with in school writing: the real and/or mixed audiences for their writing and the need to balance personal concerns with externally set requirements. Much school writing is unauthentic/unreal. Students write letters to editors which are never posted and they are expected to write to unknown examiners about deeply felt responses to literature and life. We certainly expect them to be very trusting and confident individuals. I think Tanya's positive and quick response to me was a measure of her need to feel safe in disclosing her self, as one does in creative composing. I certainly felt a need to protect her trust.

Tanya's reflective ability was apparent in her fourth interview with me where she recalled a project on Beethoven which she had done in Year 3. She said:

> I did a lot of information and I put (it) into my own words and I learnt a lot about Beethoven . . . since then I've done other projects . . . I look up words like 'tranquil'

and put an easier word so I don't take in what I'm writing. I wanted that project 'Beethoven' to be good instead of just making the teacher know I'd written it word for word so I tried to put it into my own words . . . that's why it worked.

Intuitively, Tanya articulated the theory that one learns by using one's own language in writing. Her metacognitive ability to reflect on her own learning/writing processes is characteristic of many able writers and thinkers. Tanya was so articulate about her writing that as the interviews progressed in the first six months of the study, they became more like unstructured conversations on a theme.

Towards the end of her primary schooling, Tanya was very aware of the imminent transitions to secondary school. The issue of her identity as a writer and learner was a recurring one. In reply to the difficult question I posed, 'How would you know you were getting better at writing?', Tanya replied:

> Do you mean as you get older . . . fantasy things? I think they'd have to be more realistic and not all fantasy . . . if you are writing a novel for Senior School it might be easier to do something more realistic because you know more about those things than a fantasy world. I used to like fantasy but as I've grown older I know it's not really true. I'd rather be a fantasy person than too realistic because when I write stories they seem a bit dull and dreary and too realistic.

It is hard to know whether Tanya's comments on the apparent disjunction between fantasy and realism was an accurate perception or not of different expectations of primary-school and secondary-school students, but I suspect it was. Tanya was aware of a conflict which many students must experience, albeit less consciously, as they move into adolescence and the secondary school. We know very little about the way students experience, express or resolve the apparent conflict between composing for self-development or self-exploration and writing for more external or transactional purposes. In a well-integrated writing programme the conflict should be minimized as students experience a range of writing modes, functions and audiences.

When the experimental study method shifted from interviews with the students to a more direct intervention method at the end of the first year of the project, it was not surprising that Tanya responded easily to the concentration exercises and those involving the revision of inner speech. The following examples of Tanya's writing in the intervention programme should illustrate further her abilities and preoccupations.

Tanya's writing in the intervention programme

In her first piece following a concentration exercise, at the end of Year 6, Tanya wrote:

> *Concentrating*
> Swiss mountains with snow-covered alps, the south coast of Australia with huge rocks called 'The Twelve Apostles' and the waves were pounding against them, Ayers

Rock and Mount Sinai when Moses was given the Ten Commandments. A big top hat resembling the Swiss mountains. A picture at the Art Gallery about snow covered mountains in Switzerland in a town called Sion. I was on the beach without a towel and I was lying on the sand.

I asked the students after they had done their initial writing to reflect on this writing and thinking experience. Tanya wrote:

> We had to concentrate fully on what we were thinking. We could think freely on all subjects instead of one place like in a story you can't jump from country to country thinking freely, but when you were just concentrating we could think about anything after anything instead of keeping to one subject . . . I would know more about the world if I concentrated. If someone is an actor and they read the script and they don't feel the part they're not concentrating.

Although Tanya acknowledges the freedom she experienced in writing this way, in fact there is a coherent structure in her writing. The imaginative associations between Swiss mountains, the Australian coastline and inland Ayers Rock; the historical and religious links to Moses and the cultural links with the Art Gallery have an internal logic and imagistic coherence. Tanya is 'composing the mind' (Moffett 1981b: 15). Notice how she moved from a narrative structure in recording the pictures in her mind to her final speculative comment in her reflection upon the writing process: 'I would know more about the world if I concentrated.' This reflection upon her relationship with the world shows that she has discovered a way to understand better and to structure that developing awareness. Her comment about the actor not feeling the part because he/she lacks concentration, suggests that she sees concentration and empathy (or thinking and feeling) as closely linked and complementary. It is also worth noting how integrated and flowing the movement from narrative to speculation can be.

In the second concentration exercise (at the end of Year 6), I asked the students to think about some problems they needed to solve, such as some work they were doing at school or some issue of concern. Tanya thought about a novel she had written and then outlined the plot in the report she wrote about the concentration exercise. Again, there is evidence of her metacognitive strategy in her conscious reflection upon her own thinking processes: 'I was wondering whether I would say that they explored the island . . . or whether I would have a castaway . . . I solved the problem by starting a new book.'

Tanya found this exercise harder than the previous one because she had been asked to focus on one particular issue. She preferred to range freely in her thinking, and my structuring of the exercise was probably premature.

In the second year of the project (Year 7) when the intervention programme was operating more fully, the experimental students had a number of sessions where they were encouraged to write more sustained stream-of-consciousness pieces composed after a period of concentration. Basically the method involved the students sitting quietly 'watching whatever comes to mind' and writing down those thoughts, feelings and images. To help make the transitions from thinking to composing, the students were asked to write 'I am thinking about . . .' at the top of the page and to continue writing from there. When they became stuck for words, I suggested that they rewrite that phrase and continue. Surprisingly, that simple method and the encouragement to write about the mental blocks which occurred in the writing process often carried writers over difficult stages. If difficulties are acknowledged and accepted as part of the process, they seem to lose their inhibiting power. That is, the act of writing 'I am thinking about . . .' helped reduce defences against writing.

In the first free-writing piece done in the second year of the project (Year 7), Tanya wrote for thirty-five minutes about other countries, ski-ing, trout farming and memories of family outings. The images were strongly conveyed and detailed, suggesting their significance in Tanya's emotional and cognitive life. Most significantly, there was a sense of the integrating force of writing which involves the revision of inner speech. Tanya created the impression that she was drawing together memories and images in a personally significant way. There was no overt consciousness of her meeting the externally imposed demands of a reading audience, yet the writing was powerfully communicative to a reader. Tanya had a well-internalized sense of the needs of an audience – a sense integrated with her own expressive needs so that there was no impression of compromise in her writing voice. Tanya's next piece in response to the concentration work was as follows:

> After we had landed on this weird planet some strange creatures came out and take me to their leader. I am lead to a magnificent room with a throne. At the back of this throne sits a strange creature. He makes a glass of a strange liquid and I drink it. Then I can understand what he says to me. He asks me if I came to steal his magnificent treasure but I say no. I tell him what happened to me and he takes me to a huge lavishly furnished room and there I meet the man who came up in a bubble before me. We exchange stories and I find out that from what he had overheard the strange people thought we were gods and are intending to give us a room all to ourselves and treat us with respect. We go from our room and tell them that we are not gods and they decide to have a meeting. We wait for a while and the King tells us that five of them agreed to let us go but two of them said we are gods and we must stay there to keep the city in good hands. We decide to talk to those two citizens and finally they give up and we are allowed to leave with two highly powered ships. So we both get our ships, say goodbye and leave. Almost immediately our ships turn back into bubbles and we finally arrive back at the island.

It is worth recalling here that Tanya had expressed concern towards the end of the previous year about the acceptable place of fantasy in the secondary school. It would seem from this story, and from her earlier writings, that the need to explore both the world of reality and the world of fantasy are equally powerful. Given the choice, Tanya moved across memories of reality and imagined fantasies, as the need arose. In so doing, the anchoring point for her exploration is her own place in these complementary worlds. The meaning and purpose of thought and feeling were implicitly explored through Tanya's writing. The unconscious fairy-tale echoes of her fantasy writing are a reminder of the significance of such tales in the developing psychic lives of children. Tanya spins a tale and uses narrative for the psychic purposes appropriate for a developing adolescent. She was able to draw upon resources already internalized as positive structures for self-development. In the story above she sees herself in control of her destiny.

In a more structured exercise leading to reflective writing, I asked the writers to think about a time they had learnt something new. Tanya wrote the following:

I'm thinking about learning – going to Eucembene and learning how to row the boat. The first two times I got soaked but gradually I learnt how to do it and every morning Michael and I would race down to the lake and try to get there first and I learnt how to fish for trout, not that we caught any fish and I learnt about trout, how they are born and kept alive and things like that. When we had social studies yesterday we were doing things like the great wonders of the world and it said all about the lines of Nasco and Stonehenge and the statues of Easter Island and the snakey hills of someplace.

When I was learning how to do the Rubic Cube I was taught by Skye and I got better and better and after a week I could do two faces and my record was 31 seconds for one face. In Religion this morning we were talking about nature scenes and we were telling each other about our favourite places and how we were struck by the sense of wonder. Like when we went to Eucembene we went past a big red sandhill one day and it was really beautiful because it was so typically Australian and everybody always thinks that Australia is so arid and that sandhill made me think of it. When we went down to Jervis Bay I was learning how to waterski and I just couldn't do it. Probably because it was so cold. In the night we'd play spotlight and the sand was so white and squeeky it reminded me of St Thomas (the Caribbean island where Tanya was born).

The piece needs to be quoted in full to recognize the way that writing can organize into a coherent structure a number of ideas and images significant to the writer. The process of writing about a learning experience does more than inform the reader and the writer about that process; it encourages the integration and exploration of a number of associated memories of events.

The expressive and informative description of learning to do the Rubik's Cube led into the recall of the discussion in religion class that morning where the students were 'struck by the sense of wonder'. That reflection in turn led to a more detailed exploration of memories of beautiful scenery. Though this reflective writing is primarily expressive, there is evidence of Tanya using her observations of the world to test a commonly held hypothesis – 'that Australia is so arid'. As a whole the piece functions as a mix of description, narrative and reflection. It functions for the writer to integrate a number of aspects of experience in ways appropriate to the writer's needs. There is a need to structure experience in particular ways, through story, description and reflection in order for the writer to perceive their pattern and their significance. This happened unconsciously when Tanya responded to the suggestion that she think about a time she learnt something. The open-ended nature of the writing task allowed the ordering and patterning to follow the writer's internal organization.

In Tanya's piece here we see the rudiments of speculative thinking and can sense the emotional impact of a sense of wonder. This integration of thought and feeling is, arguably, a mark of development as a writer, just as it is an important part of the process of development.

Shortly after Tanya wrote the piece above, the focus of the intervention programme moved from writing primarily for self to exchanging letters with the experimental students in the other experimental school. The experimental students in the two schools were naturally, and mutually, curious. They were eager to find peer audiences for their writing: a spontaneous outcome of the kinds of writing for self (and for me) which they had been doing in the intervention programme to date.

In the quite arbitrary pairing between the experimental students in the two schools, Tanya's writing partner was Lino, a very pleasant boy of Italian descent. Lino came along cheerfully to the writing sessions but he had great difficulty in concentrating on writing. His mind was on soccer much of the time. There was pressure on him from home to succeed at school but success in maths was his prime motivation. He rarely read books or newspapers but he liked to write stories about vampires. His interest in stories was largely a carry-over from his primary-school experience, as was his willingness on some occasions to redraft a story. In terms of intellectual development and social maturity, Tanya and Lino were at opposite ends of the spectrum. Needless to say, they had no information about each other apart from what was revealed in their exchange of letters.

Tanya wrote the first letter in the exchange and she outlined her biographical details, her hobbies and school subjects. Her most expressive comment came at the end of the letter when she wrote '. . . sorry if I've bored you to death.'

This kind of comment was such a predominant feature of the letters between the experimental students that I analysed the letters for what I have termed 'self-esteem' comments: comments which function for the writer to seek self-endorsement from the reader, or which function to endorse the reader's self-esteem (Arnold 1983). Tanya and most of the experimental writers recognized intuitively that their initial letters had to be more than a catalogue of information, if there were to be the establishment of a mutual relationship between the writers. Self-esteem comments do not feature in most school writing because the teacher/reader is not perceived as someone with whom to develop a relationship through writing. The writers here saw their letters as having real communicative potential and they drew on their implicit knowledge of human relationships to develop that potential.

Understandably, Tanya's second letter to Lino was more relaxed than the first. She thanked Lino for his letter in which he had written 'I've liked your letter very much and your letter never bored me a bit. I just hope I never bored you.' Their mutual recognition of anxiety about being boring helped to establish some trust in the relationship. Lino had great difficulty writing his letters to Tanya as he had little idea what to write about. Once he missed a writing session to go to a maths class and then returned to the group at the end and scribbled out a brief note. Tanya replied, 'Thank you for your letter but I would appreciate it if you would write longer letters.' She then unconsciously modelled for him how he might write at length by describing her music camp and other events. In acknowledgement of Lino's interests, she asked him what football team he followed, adding 'I don't really like any but if I had to choose I'd pick . . .' Her attempt to show interest in him had a dual purpose; it was essential for Lino to keep writing in order for their exchange to continue and Tanya was learning to balance her own expressive needs with the needs of her reader. In a mutual exchange of writing there is skill involved in making the writing function for both the writer's and the reader's purposes. Interestingly, Tanya's veiled reproach to Lino in her request for longer letters gave him an opportunity to apologize and to explain that he had to do his maths:

> Sorry, I haven't written . . . I hope you forgive me . . . Today I'll try to write a lot I try to write as much as I can because next we got Maths . . . I hope you like what I write today, and the next few weeks I'll try to make my letters a bit more interesting.

The whole letter was an extended apology and Tanya became bored with Lino, just as he feared. Because there developed an uneven number of experimental students between the two schools, I gave Tanya another writer, as well as Lino, with whom to exchange letters. There was a break for the August vacation, then Lino took up writing to Tanya again. His first letter after the break started, 'I liked reading your letters.' Following my suggestion he then wrote about what he found easy or hard about writing. He said he liked writing stories on space and horror best but 'letters are my second best (kind) of writing.'

Although Tanya's progress is the prime focus here, aspects of her ability as a writer are reflected in the ways she found to help Lino, a reluctant writer. Both she and Lino relied heavily on self-esteem comments to help them over the difficult parts of their writing exchange. Tanya had better resources than he did for writing elaborated letters, but Lino could respond to help when Tanya or I offered it. Even when Lino wrote very little, Tanya thanked him for his letter, adding on one occasion, 'don't worry about writing much if it's too much sacrifice.' A breakthrough occurred for Lino when I suggested he write Tanya a story. He wrote the longest letter so far (thirty-five lines) outlining what he called 'one of the best stories I've ever written' – a story about Blacula, Lino's version of the Dracula theme. Again at the end Lino wrote, 'sorry if my letter was boring'. He certainly had a sense of a real audience for his story/letter.

Tanya responded favourably: 'I did not think that your letter was boring. I thought (it) was interesting. I will now tell you a story of my own.' Once they were both comfortable with the relationship again they could proceed with their own writing. In terms of relative writing ability the relationship was very uneven, but Tanya's ability to help Lino through his difficulties with her endorsing comments of him and her practical suggestions, in turn allowed her the freedom to explore her own experiences through her letters to him. When given the choice, Tanya wrote most graphically about her early life experiences. Although such accounts served a primary function for her of allowing her to evaluate those experiences through their retelling, they made interesting reading too. Tanya was at a stage in her writing development where she could write effectively and simultaneously for herself, interested peer and adult readers. She had some sense of a universal audience in her story telling and ordered her narrative in a logical time sequence with appropriate degrees of descriptive detail.

Tanya continued to encourage Lino through her letters by her positive responses and by suggesting ways they could keep the exchange going: 'I've got an idea, instead of writing letters we can write stories about whatever we want.' Tanya was not entirely disinterested in using the technique of positive reinforcement. Once she had dealt with Lino's ego in her letters she was able to follow her own inclinations and write about whatever suited her. There was sufficient flexibility in her writing methods for her to deal with several issues in the same letter. Tanya made a revealing comment in one of her letters: 'Yes I care very much if I don't get good marks in class because my parents expect a lot from me.'

In the last year of the study the issue of Tanya's expectations of herself and her parents' expectation of her became a more open conflict about which she sought my counselling. She felt isolated from her peers because her learning interests and reading were more mature than those of her friends. She was developing faster intellectually and emotionally than many of her peers and some of her school lessons failed to stimulate her. On the surface her relationships with her peers were amiable and unconflicted but there was often a sense of urgency in her as she wrote in the intervention writing classes; as if this were a valuable chance to write out the accumulated images in her inner speech.

By the end of the second year of the study (Year 7), Tanya's stories and letters showed her ability to use autobiographical material and memories and observations as part of a communication to either a special audience, her writing partner or a more general audience. She was able to balance the wish to be egocentric in a letter by detailing personal experiences with the capacity to show awareness of the reader's need for detail and for acknowledgement. In fiction, the writer's need to work out some psychic structure through the story is often obscured by the story itself. As readers we do not know clearly which parts of the writer's self are consciously or unconsciously projected into the characters. Partly because of this, the structure of fictional narrative writing can provide a healthy defence strategy for the exploration of the writer's psychic issues. In letter writing the writer's self is more clearly exposed and both writer and reader may be aware of this.

Tanya's suggestion to Lino that they write stories to each other was possibly a recognition of this vulnerability and of his preferences, as well as an implicit recognition of the power of narrative to make safely conscious what is often unconscious.

The final letter for Year 7 which Tanya wrote to Lino she outlined a character, John, whom she was planning to put into a science fiction story. She listed John's favourite foods and detailed his best quality: 'he doesn't put himself before others. People like him because he's smart and he's nice to people ... The adventures he has are saving people from the perils of space.' In figurative language Tanya was projecting her own view of a hero figure into her character. By making up a story about him she could control the outcome of his adventures and test her own hypothesis about the fate of such characters. In this way, certain kinds of highly imagined narrative can serve as the precursors to speculative thought.

Although it is possible to detect stages of growth across very broad spectrums of discourse, for example, from writing wholly for self to writing to generalized others, or from writing a narrative of recorded events to writing a narrative with hypothetical possibilities (like George Orwell's *1984*), what is often perceptible in the work of a writer over a period of time are the rudiments of development prior to their fuller expression. That is, in the psychodynamic spiral theory, there is a basic cohesiveness in the growth of discourse where one kind of discourse carries within it the embryonic forms of other kinds of discourse. For example, in the piece quoted earlier, Tanya commented on a big red sandhill which she thought was really beautiful even though everyone 'always thinks that Australia is so arid'. Here an observation lead to a rudimentary form of theorizing – that sandhills can be beautiful even though they are usually associated with arid areas (Eucembene is a non-arid area), or that sandhills also appear in non-arid areas, or that aridity can still be beautiful. Obviously Tanya did not explore fully the implications of her comment but the basic theorizing structure is evident.

There is a less complex cause–effect relationship explicated in the same piece of writing when Tanya writes, 'I was learning how to waterski and I just couldn't do it. Probably because it was so cold.' While the cause–effect relationship might operate as a rationalization for her inability to learn a new skill, it shows, none the less, the functioning of explicit causal relationships. At a lower level of development such relationships are inexplicit and unconscious. A further stage of development for Tanya would be for her to be aware of the possibility that she is using rationalization as a psychological defence. While it is possible to detect instances of growth within whole discourses, it is harder to classify discourses as whole pieces of, for example, theoretical writing, especially in the early years of secondary school. One piece of writing might function at several levels for the writer and it helps if we can analyse a writer's growth over several years, picking up important, but maybe isolated, examples of higher levels of thinking and language.

In the third year of the study (Year 8) Tanya's writing in the intervention programme became more allegorical as she recounted her dreams in her letters to Lino, and retold the story of Oscar Wilde's 'The Happy Prince'. The detail in the retelling of the dreams and the Happy Prince story was appropriately elaborated to make interesting reading in itself. Tanya made no attempt to analyse why the dreams and story were personally significant but she wrote about them at some length. The individual ordering of the dreams and the story served some function in allowing her to create her own version. The dreams and the story were evocative experiences with complex metaphoric structures in their own right. Tanya did justice to these structures in her own retelling, though she was, presumably, not able to explore more explicitly their significance for her. None the less, she responded to their metaphoric and emotional complexity and needed to make those sources her own through her written language.

For writers like Tanya who pattern experiences through their own discourses, there are plenty of primary sources in everyday life. It is possible that Tanya's retelling of the Happy Prince story served as a model for the kind of writing which fuses thought and feeling in an allegorical form. At particular stages of emotional and cognitive development, in childhood, adolescence and adulthood, fairy tales, allegories, myths, science fiction stories and poetic writing can all serve the purpose of synthesizing complex views of reality into well-integrated, extended metaphors. Within such metaphors, thought and feeling are cohesive, balanced, and often implicit within the ordering of images and events. The reader is then able to project his/her own view of reality, to test it against the reality of the story and to reorganize, evaluate and perhaps internalize some aspects of the reading experience. In this way, the reading and writing of narratives, especially those with a deep emotional structure afford some experience of implicit hypothesis testing. The links between narrative and argument and the ways developing writers make transitions between them are explored in *Narrative and Argument*, Richard Andrews (ed.) (1989).

Tanya continued to write stories and reflective pieces recalling her fantasies and wishes about living in other countries, and letters to Lino for the rest of the third year of the study (Year 8). Towards the end of that year she wrote a particularly interesting letter to Lino in which she retold the story of a book she had read recently. She took thirty-one lines to retell the story of Debbie, a schizophrenic girl who had spent three years 'in a looney asylum'. Debbie lived in two different worlds, Ur and Earth: 'the two worlds couldn't come together or else she'd go crazy.' Then Debbie talked to a psychologist and gradually 'got more sane and human', until he went away and she started burning herself. The psychologist returned, Debbie improved, 'left the place and did an equivalent of the HSC [Higher School Certificate examination at the end of secondary school] and she passed it.' The story does not end there: Debbie had another mental breakdown and had to return to the asylum where 'everyone there was mad at her because she had failed in the outside world.' However, at last Debbie said goodbye to the elders of Ur, 'so it was really a hopeful ending, now that she didn't have Ur, she could be sane. Anyway it was an unreal book.'

Tanya's recounting of the story of Debbie was particularly significant in the light of the theme which emerged in her own writing and thinking from the beginning of the study and continued throughout it: how to reconcile the apparently opposing worlds of thinking and feeling, of fantasy and reality, of individualism and comformity. No doubt Tanya identified with Debbie who could not reconcile her two opposing worlds, even though she was helped by talking with an understanding adult. In the end Debbie had to say 'goodbye to all the elders of Ur' which led to what Tanya described as 'a hopeful ending'. In spite of all her difficulties, Debbie was able to take charge of her own life. I do not know the source of Tanya's story but her response to it seemed to mirror, at least in part, a conflict in her own developing sense of identity. In her writing and her conversations with me Tanya often referred to her own dreams and fantasies, describing them as 'weird'. She was worried that others would see her as 'a bit crazy' because she was so much in touch with her own imaginative thinking. For Tanya, the story of Debbie offered similar possibilities for identification and conflict-solving which fairy tales offer younger readers.

Although Tanya knew at heart that her fantasies and dreams added richly to her inner world, she needed reassurance from time to time that the rational and irrational aspects of her thinking and experiencing were integrated in her core ego. Tanya recognized the difference between stories which offer a rich, complex view of life and imagination, and those which underestimate the active, engaged reader/viewer. (She had made disparaging comments to Lino about the story line in the musical, *Half a Sixpence*.) In the implicit evaluation of her own inner world evident in the letter about the Debbie story, Tanya seemed confident about the basic stability of the cognitive and affective, the literal and the metaphoric aspects of her mind. In the same piece of writing she could move easily across broad spectrums of thinking, while exploring implicitly significant and developing aspects of her self. Tanya had a well-established and integrated ability to respond personally and effectively to literature and life through her writing. She was in a strong position to develop a more highly organized and sensitive analysis and synthesis of experience because she knew how writing can function for personal and public purposes. Moffett (1976: 460) makes the point that while growth in the literal modes of discourse proceeds up the ladder from the here-now to the there-then,

> it is in the nature of disguised psychic material that one symbolizes it first in the there-then and only gradually comes to represent it in explicitly personal terms . . . as regards . . . unconscious psychic life (a person) moves along a continuum that begins in the far-fetched, with things remote from him in time and space and works backward toward himself.

This kind of movement contradicts the commonly held assumption underlying much secondary-school writing, that literal modes of writing need to take precedence over metaphoric modes. In the case of a student like Tanya who could operate equally well in both, the fear that fantasy and metaphor had to be put aside in the secondary school caused her a certain amount of conscious anxiety. This was partly worked through in her own reading, writing and talking.

From the evidence I collected in the writing survey and from my observations in the school, it is unlikely that Tanya's need to write about her dreams and her personal responses to her reading and life experiences could have been met in her regular class writing. She might have been able to do some of it through journal writing, but she needed the sense of an interested reader responding to her writing in order to continue it. In fact, it mattered very little whether I commented on her work as long as she had a sense of an interested reader to provide an image towards whom she could direct her edited inner speech. As Tanya became more conscious of the world of her own mind, and conscious of her own power to organize it and evaluate it through writing, she moved towards increasingly more abstract and differentiated forms of discourse. She began to experiment imaginatively with historical time and fictional time.

In her contribution to a Christmas journal which each experimental group wrote and collated to exchange between themselves at the end of the third year of the study (Year 8), Tanya wrote the following:

Fantasy

I went into the past last Thursday and I went back to the Russian civil war between Catherine and Peter the Third. I was in a narrow side street and I saw on the main road, a group of people gathering and talking in whispers. I heard a few words like 'overthrow the queen'. . . 'a revolution is the only thing'. . . 'the queen is insane'. On the fringes of the group I saw a small man, huddled in his clothes to keep the cold out – or to hide his face. I noticed that he was busy writing something down. So when the group broke up, I followed the man at a safe distance and when he approached a door, I walked into him and knocked his book flying. I pretended to be sorry and went to pick the book up and unseen by him I ripped the page out – I then watched him go and, when he was out of sight, I looked at the paper. It contained the directions for the conspirators to overthrow the queen. I quickly made my way to the Winter Palace where Catherine was. I told the footman that I had to see the queen, but at first they wouldn't let me in since I didn't have a pass, then the queen appeared, asked who was making the noise, so I quickly darted forward and told her all about the plot, and showed the paper. She ordered the people coming onto the Palace to be searched, and on the third day we found the conspirator and quickly, all the men in the plot were arrested and so the queen was saved. I went back to normal time and learnt all about it in modern history a few weeks later.

By placing herself within the historical events Tanya was able to identify with an event remote in time and distance from her own life. In her own imaginative recreation story she managed to overcome that historical distance by characterizing people and events. My conversations with Tanya satisfied me that Tanya had intuitively learnt about history by recreating her own version in imaginative writing. She had experimented with the potential 'timelessness' of fictional writing, thereby symbolizing the universality of experience.

Tanya's responses at the end of the third year of my study to a sentence completion task which I designed to elicit the experimental students' attitudes to writing reveal more about her feeling and self-concept as a writer. She completed the sentence 'When I am asked to write in class I feel . . .', with, 'uncertain because sometimes I can't put into proper words the information I'm supposed to be writing.' Yet in response to the sentence, 'Since I have been coming to (the research) class I . . .', she wrote, 'have enjoyed writing more and I feel much better about writing in class.'

It would seem that Tanya's earlier reference to putting into proper words the information she is supposed to be writing relates to the kinds of transactional writing which students have to do in many of their school subjects. A further response reveals more about this perceived difficulty: she completed the sentence, 'Good writers are able to . . .' with 'write what they want without feeling worried and give a clear picture of what they are saying.' She also wrote that the best help she could get with her writing was 'when I am writing something for myself instead of for other people.'

Tanya felt very keenly the need to conform to some imposed model of writing, even though she was accomplished in many kinds of discourse before she became part of the study. Her stories and note-making in Year 6 showed an ability to sustain narrative, to write embedded sentences, to define causal relationships and to convey thoughts and feelings with clarity, sensitivity and precision. Of letter-writing tasks such as she had undertaken in the research study, Tanya wrote '[I feel . . .] sometimes happy, sometimes annoyed because if I am writing to Lino, I can write what I feel but if I'm writing to a pen pal, I have to be sort of formal', so the problem of writing to some perceived expectations was not confined to formal school writing. For Tanya it seems to relate more to writing situations where she feels too distant from the reader and the purpose of the writing. As long as she had a sense of an interested and accepting reader to whom the writing could be focused, the problem disappeared. Even though Tanya had never met Lino, and he rarely commented specifically on the content of her letters, his apologies and excuses for not writing regularly and at length to her at least served the purpose of providing a continuing sense of a sympathetic peer audience.

In the final year of the study, Year 9, Tanya's writing became more confident. Though her inner concerns such as her dreams, her self-image, her peer relationships and her home and school life were repeated themes in her writing, there was a more explicit concern for the state of the world around her. She had always had a concern about her own freedom to express herself, but now there was emerging a sense of concern for others. As a warm-up exercise to extended writing in the final year of the study, I asked the experimental students to write down whatever words/ideas/associations came to mind when they heard certain words. In response to 'anger', Tanya wrote, 'injustice, rebellious, unfair teachers, prison camp, overpowering, insecure'. In response to 'my ideal self', she wrote, 'fun, but smart, fun to be with, thoughtful, hard working, never excusing myself, self-disciplined'. The writers then chose one of the ideas the exercise had generated to expand into a sustained piece of writing. Tanya wrote about people who annoy her. Such people were those who complained about little things. From her reading of books like *The Great Escape*, *The Wooden Horse*, *Hanged in Auschwitz* and other books about prisoner-of-war camps in the Second World War, she had been inspired by men who survived the most unspeakable, horrific things and yet they all seem to be pretty religious and courageous, giving up things for others. She was impressed with one survivor of Gestapo torture who 'never sounds bitter about it: it's very grim, but he survived and is a better person for it. He doesn't boast about anything'. Tanya's sensitive response to her reading and her capacity for identification and empathy provide her with opportunities for exploring, evaluating and integrating her own developing view of the world, involving the past, present and future.

Tanya was working here towards a 'morality of self-accepted moral principles', in Kohlberg's terms (quoted in Wilkinson *et al*. 1980: 63). From her reading and life experiences she was working out for herself a set of moral principles. Her irritation with people who complain about 'little things' is understandable in the context of the powerful emotional impact her war books had on her. However, she does not yet recognize the unequal relativity of her judgements. That is, she fails to see the possibility that people can be both annoyed about minor irritations and as outraged as she is about the gross injustices of concentration camps. It is interesting to note how Tanya's strong subjective responses to her reading stimulated her reflections upon moral principles. This is clearly not the case with all readers and writers, as many responses to the *Kes* story showed. In Tanya's case she was emotionally, psychologically and cognitively ready to make transitions between various kinds of experience.

Tanya's earlier self-reflections and her expressed wish to be self-disciplined, popular with her peers and aware of her inner world and outer reality, are precursors, in part, to the kinds of affective, cognitive, social and moral development which became more explicit in her writing in the final year of the study. I say, 'in part', because obviously family relationships, attitudes and influences are extremely powerful long before the child develops literacy. None the less, I think we can see in Tanya's writing over time, evidence in her focused and edited inner speech of her self-development. That is, we can see how her expressiveness and her reflections are patterned and integrated through her writing. I think it is reasonable to infer that this patterning process can influence the development of an individual whose behaviour and beliefs are functionally integrated with the self and its environment. Clearly there are many ways self-development occurs other than through writing, but with writing and other recorded forms of creative expression we can at least analyse the product and, as in Tanya's case, record some of the process.

I will illustrate this point with an analysis of a story Tanya wrote in the final year of the study. The story was about a Saturday night in the life of a surgeon in an emergency accident ward of a busy hospital. What was noticeable about the story was not so much its accurate scene setting as the human-interest vignettes contained within it. The third paragraph began:

The waiting room was thick with smoke: worried mothers, fathers, brothers, friends, etc., none of them believing it could've happened to them. The hot rod kid's father was here with a smelly cigar and angry voice, not believing that his Johnny could do something like that: he was a politician. Surprisingly though, a real mouse of a lady (mother of someone) told him in a sharp voice where to go. He was so surprised he didn't say another thing, just sat there with his mouth hanging out.

The story continued with details of events and interpolations of extended character observations. The crux of the story, which extended to seventy lines in all, concerned the surgeon/narrator saving the life of the tennis star, John McEnroe, after much bullying from the star's agent and interference from newspaper reporters:

> Mr McEnroe was lucky that he wasn't damaged for life. A lesser surgeon might have botched the job, but I was just lucky because my adrenalin kept me going. I was just relaxing, having a cigarette in my own little room at the hospital when the agent came in. He looked much relieved and couldn't stop thanking me. He apologised for his recent behaviour, because he was fond of John and didn't want to see him hurt. I just marvelled that anyone could stay as nice as that, with a friek like John McEnroe for a client. He even invited me over for dinner to celebrate, but I declined and returned home to my flat and ate a quiet dinner on my own. My spirits were restored and I felt thankful that I'd been able to help someone.

One of the notable features of this story was Tanya's ability to order events as well as to indicate and account for changes in the feelings of the narrator. Unlike earlier, less mature narratives, the events serve as a backdrop to the implicit characterization of the narrator. As the narrator/surgeon, her anxieties about her work, her feelings, her attitudes towards the patients and her observations of the people in the emergency ward were foreshadowed in a sustained, consistently focused point of view. One shortcoming of the story was that we never learn what John McEnroe's operation was for. From the build-up of tensions throughout the story (the crowd of people, the behaviour of individuals, the threats of court action from the star's agent, the harassment from reporters), the story became primarily focused on one particular interaction; that between the surgeon and her internal responses to her patient. In the final paragraph the atmosphere becomes reflective and calm. The narrator's sense of ethical and social satisfaction transcends the earlier feelings of dislike for the patient. Another aspect of experience had been explored and resolved by the writer through her narrative: 'My spirits were restored and I felt thankful that I's been able to help someone.' The voice of the altruistic adolescent resonates here.

The fact that there is a somewhat idealized view of a surgeon's response to an operation does not matter. The changes in the pace and tensions of the narrative, and the insights into the narrator's feelings and motivations that the reader can share create plausibility. While the story functions in important ways for the writer, the reader's needs for details, logical sequencing and the patterning of events are rarely overlooked. Thoughts and feelings are balanced, events and characters fit cohesively into the structure. And Tanya's writing voice sounds authentic and integrated. Comments like 'Surprisingly though', 'I've never liked newspaper reporters', 'The reporters loved that (the threat of litigation) and I could see them reaching for their notebooks', suggest a feeling of intimacy between the writer and her intended audience. She is confident that the reader is sympathetic to her point of view.

This level of control in narrative writing is mature for a Year 9 writer (fourteen years old) and is possibly within the top level of achievement one could expect for narrative writing at this stage. It is sometimes difficult to detect growth in writing even over a four-year period but comparisons between similar kinds of writing such as narratives based on personal experience and narratives based on imagined experience can be illuminating. I think we can see an expansion of narrative techniques across Tanya's stories. In particular, by the middle of the final year of the study, her flexibility in style, her empathy with her intended audience, her ability to make explicit what is necessary and to keep implicit what demands subtlety, are marks of her writing ability. Just as convincing are her increased ability to differentiate, to write figuratively and metaphorically, to write with a sense of engagement with the subject and the audience, and, finally, to remain centred in the writing experience.

Tanya's reasons for continually choosing narratives for the explorations of a number of personal and cognitive issues are not clear. That mode seemed to offer her a rich resource for her writing development and was consistently her choice in the intervention programme. I do not know whether she moved into explicit argument or theorizing later in her school years. It is possible that the truncation she experienced between most of her school writing and her own experiences of the functional potential of more personal and expressive writing motivated her to work within the narrative mode while exploring its possibilities to extend her insights into herself and her world.

Although Tanya's test writing showed development over the four-year period, the writing she did in the intervention programme was clearly more richly revealing of her flexibility with language and her creativity in language and thinking. It also revealed something of the ways writing can function to foster and pattern self-awareness. It is illuminating to analyse Tanya's test writing in the light of what was revealed by the case-study analyses.

Tanya's test writing

Tanya's results for her test writing, marked holistically, and marked by criteria, are shown in table 4.1

Tanya's test writing, and her intervention-programme writing both showed signs of development over the four-year period. As well as comparing her scores across the four years, it is worth comparing her *Space* and *Future* letters to see some of the features of her developmental trend. Her *Space* letter showed her ability to write personally and expressively but with a concomitant awareness of a general audience. She was able to differentiate writing into both prose and poetry in that letter as well as demonstrate the effective use of both within it. She outlined the features of blank verse and offered her own illustration of it. Her

Table 4.1   Tanya's test writing results
(a) Holistic marking (averages of the marks awarded by markers
A and B)

SCALE	Space	Peer	Kes	Principal	Future
(8)	6	6	5	7	4

(b) Criteria marking (averages of the marks awarded by Markers
A and B)

	Space	Peer	Kes	Principal	Future
Audience (3)	2	2	3	3	3
Creativity (5)	3	1	2.5	2.5	5
Thinking (6)	4	3	4	5	6
Language (6)	3	3	4	5	6

informative, engaging letter to the spaceman indicated her own insights into writing processes and into the value of reporting facts in one's own words.

Tanya's *Future* letter and her outline of the features of different hypothetical careers showed her now increased ability to differentiate thought and language. Her future life was highly imagined with teasingly inexplicit references to the hypothetical discovery of a new metal. Her ability to move back and forwards in time, speculating on the possibilities of her future life was an echo of the same ability she showed in her Catherine the Great story quoted earlier. She knew when to be succinct and when to be explicit; she was self-aware and other-aware, and she created the impression that she could use language flexibly to explore, to integrate and to communciate experience.

As far as the intervention writing programme was concerned, Tanya's development as a writer occurred in a fairly non-directive way. I did spend considerable time talking with her about various issues and ideas, both in the sessions and outside. Whatever the intervention programme contributed to Tanya's writing development occurred largely through the relationships it offered her with her writing partners, with me, and indeed with her own inner world, and through the opportunities she had to develop more fully those abilities which were present latently, or in partly developed form, at the beginning of the study. It is probable that the main effect of the intervention programme was to allow Tanya to explore and work through issues relevant to her psychic and cognitive development to which there was insufficient attention given in the normal school routine.

Mindful of Tanya's expressed concern in Year 6 about a perceived conflict between rational and imaginative thought in secondary-school contexts, we can speculate that Tanya's creative potential might not have been developed without the encouragement she was offered in the intervention programme to use effectively both kinds of thinking and writing. Tanya was astute enough, even in Year 6, to match her learning approaches to perceived teacher expectations but her psychic and cognitive development needed a full range of expressive opportunities.

Summary

- I think this case study of Tanya supports the argument that, for certain able writers, contexts which endorse them as writers and support their struggles to make meaning and to communicate it provide a stimulus for growth.
- For less able writers contexts for writing need to be equally enabling, but also more structured.
- Tanya's case illustrates, and I hope, supports my argument about the psychodynamic nature of writing development: that writers who can be put in touch with the resources of their inner speech, sense the awareness of a positively mirroring audience and structure their thinking and feeling in expressive writing will, over a period of time, differentiate their thinking and writing for more distanced audiences and purposes.

Postscript

My relationship with Tanya did not end with the completion of the study. Early in the year following its completion Tanya wrote to me thanking me for my help and telling me that she had won a prize in English. She wrote: 'I don't feel so incompetent about writing now.' Such is the self-effacement of some talented students! In the same letter she enclosed a poem about loneliness written during the intervention programme and the comment:

> The situation at school isn't bad anymore. That time I talked to you at school it really helped: I don't bottle things up inside me anymore and I'm more ready to talk things out now, or I just write down what's bothering me. At first I wrote everything I felt, but then I started writing it in poetry and paragraphs.

Tanya asked me to reply and 'tell me what you think'. She wanted to continue her dialogues with me but she also had a sufficiently well-internalized sense of my justified belief in her abilities to use her writing as a source for dialogue with herself and with others. Tanya's writing was richly expressive of her inner life with all its hopes and conflicts. She provides us with illuminating evidence of some of the self-developing potential of a particular range of authentic composing experiences.

5 Jane and Anna: an enabling relationship between two good writers

I have selected Jane (school A) and Anna (school B) as case studies because each was a writer who showed development over the four years of the study, and together they offer insights into both the nature of the intervention writing programme and a significant peer relationship developed by the letter-writing exchange.

Although the letter-writing partners were randomly chosen, it happened that Jane and Anna were very similar in their personality, dramatic flair and positive attitudes to school and life. Both came from Italian backgrounds; Jane was a second-generation Australian, while Anna's parents were Italian born. Jane's father was a specialist doctor and Anna's a concreter. Both mothers worked at home duties.

Rapport between Jane and Anna was established very easily in their early letters. The strategies they both used to develop their relationship beyond its initial phase show us some of the psychological processes involved in writing development, especially those relevant to the establishment of relationships.

Both writers were well attuned to their own self-esteem needs and to those of others. As well, both writers established an easy, mutually enjoyable relationship with me.

I will outline some relevant information about each writer separately, then I will analyse the nature of the relationship they established and maintained through their letters.

Jane's development as a writer over the four years was at a high level. On the sum of averaged scores (average of two markers), summed over the four criteria on *Space*, *Peer*, *Kes*, *Principal* and *Future*, Jane's score for *Space* was 10 out of a possible 20 and on *Future* it was 19 out of a possible 20. Anna's score on *Space* was 10, the same as Jane's, and on *Future* her score was 15. Both writers showed development over the four years but Jane's was clearly more marked than Anna's. Over the period of the study Jane wrote twenty-two letters and eight free-association reflective pieces and Anna wrote twenty-four letters and nine free-association reflective pieces in the intervention writing programme. Within their letters both wrote a couple of poems.

Jane – an overview

From her first interview with me in Year 6, Jane's easy manner and established interest in writing attracted my attention. She was reflective about her writing processes and spoke about the relationship she perceived between reading, talking and writing. She was a keen reader and professed to being sometimes excited about writing in school (and sometimes not). She discussed with me the need she saw to provide detail in her writing, and she could differentiate some of the differences between public and private writing. She was not in the habit of keeping a writing journal but expressed interest in doing so. However, the free-association writing activities and the letter-writing exchange provided her with the personal writing she liked so she did not take up the idea of journal writing. In an interview after she had written her *Space* letter in Year 6, Jane revealed her awareness of the need to decentre in the process of writing when she told me how she faced difficulties in writing: 'Depends what you are writing about. I'd think of all the things somebody would want to know . . . if I was that person what I'd want to know.'

Consciously Jane used her reading as a source for writing ideas and she noted down words from her books which she would like to use. She mentioned the need to use imagination in writing and her own need to write 'realistically'. Interestingly, by that she meant that she reread her writing to check its effectiveness in conveying her intended meaning, rather than its factual content. Jane wrote that free-association/concentration writing activities were helpful 'Because your thinking is the most important thing in the world.'

In a later, more structured reflective piece, 'Thinking about a learning experience' Jane chose to comment on her *Space* letter. She wrote:

> I had to write about a space visitor and tell him about our writing at school. It was rather hard to find things to tell about. It would be easier now because I understand my writing more. I solved the problem by putting myself in his place and pretending I didn't know about writing and then I wrote what I would have wanted to know.

By the end of the first year of the study (Year 6) it was clear that Jane was an able writer with an interest in reflecting on her life experiences and on the place of writing in enabling her to express her thoughts and feelings. At the same time she demonstrated effective strategies for making her writing accessible to others. Jane was enthusiastic about free-association writing and on one occasion she wrote for an hour and a half, completing 150 lines of writing. She wrote about all kinds of events in her life; then she commented on her own composing:

> I suppose our imagination is set free but when we write here it is just our minds and more ourselves. It is all totally free and easy . . . I enjoy doing this. It is rather relaxing in a way and it sort of gets things off your mind. I mean it's nice to tell somebody things that happen to you especially the happy ones. It's sort of like writing a letter to a friend but even that is a bit harder because you are still not as free to write what you like. I think it is an interesting thing to do. It helps you to know yourself better because you see your thoughts in true print. It is interesting.

Jane's spontaneously expressed insights into this writing process highlight its potentially self-revealing nature. The process of reflecting thought and feeling in an expressive writing experience can then become self-generating. As Jane expressed it:

> What kept me going is the fact that I have a lot to say and when somebody says something even if it is not concerned with it your mind just clicks and I think of something new even though I've thought that there was nothing more to write.

Although Jane's writing here is clearly self-expressive, there is a strong sense, sometimes acknowledged, that she is writing for both herself and an interested audience. She correctly assumes that there is a reader interested in her mind and she is unselfconscious about sharing her thoughts. This can be attributed partly to Jane's open, confident personality and partly to her need to know she could hold another's attention. Prior to these writing experiences, Jane's class teacher had confided to me that Jane was annoying her, and the other students, with her incessant talking in class. The expressive-writing activities provided some outlet for her. When Jane found Anna as a writing partner, the problem abated sufficiently to avoid further adverse comment. Jane herself was aware that she often talked incessantly but her sense of humour, energy, intelligence and self-awareness provided a counter balance.

Anna – an overview

Like Jane, Anna had an outgoing personality, a sense of humour and a desire to do well at school. As well, she enjoyed writing and reading and believed in the value of her imagination. Generally she wrote quickly and at some length, with an awareness of the need to make sense but with some disregard for punctuation or paragraphing.

In her free-association activities, Anna did not write at great length like Jane and, at first, she seemed to be resisting the experience. In her third free-association piece, Anna wrote that she found the task 'A bit confusing because at times you think silly things too stupid to tell.' Later in the same piece she wrote more about her vulnerability in expressing herself and commented: 'when you are alone you think about all sorts of things . . . things that upset me, people who hurt my feelings.' She also expressed the wish to be friends with everyone and to lead 'one happy life with(out) misery like I do each time people talk about me and start a fight and upset me.' In the exchange of letters between Anna and Jane they shared confidences about their current personal worries. Anna needed more structure than Jane in her writing activities, but she became more open and expressive when there was a clear audience and purpose for her writing. Unlike Jane, Anna at this point had not found pleasure in elaborating her thoughts in writing. She was not yet ready to take risks. None the less, she described the free-association writing experiences as 'talking to myself or thinking to myself in my mind.'

Anna liked the structure provided by opening phrases like 'What would happen if . . .'. She followed that phrase with a speculation on the consequences of people walking backwards or shrinking, following through her ideas with an outline of the expected consequences. However, the major part of her writing was an accretion of detail rather than an extended elaboration upon consequences. At this point Jane was thinking with greater depth about her ideas, whereas Anna was still in the habit of adding details in a relatively unrelated and unsynthesized way. Differences in thinking differentiation were marked between Anna and Jane which largely account for the relative differences in their long-term writing development.

The letter-writing exchange between Jane and Anna

Jane wrote the first letter in the exchange with a fairly conventional letter to Anna in which she introduced herself and outlined some biographical details and her school subjects. Anna's first letter in reply was very lengthy and detailed, with several rhetorical questions inviting Jane to give more information about herself and her family. Anna expressed the hope that Jane would not mind, 'how messy the letter is'. Jane's letter in reply was more open and relaxed than her introductory letter. She responded sensitively to Anna's apparent interest in her and wrote 50 lines in reply. Apart from elaborating upon her own Italian background, she expressed the hope that Anna's argument with a school friend (detailed in Anna's previous letter) had been resolved, and she also apologized for her messy letter. In essence the letter was a blend of personal information and comments designed to express Jane's interest in her writing partner. In her first letter, Jane had simply signed her name. In her second letter she signed 'Your friend' and in her third letter 'Your good friend'. Even ritualistic language can reflect changes.

From the start of the letter exchange, Jane and Anna were skilled in developing friendships and concerned about maintaining them. Their sociability and their enthusiastic personalities made the formation of friendships relatively easy but also potentially volatile. In their early letters to each other they transferred from speech to writing the rhetorical strategies of endorsing each other's sense of worth by asking rhetorical questions, by apologizing for the appearance of their letters, by referring back to information given in previous letters and by seeking endorsement from each other. In her third letter, Jane thanked Anna for her long letter and apologized for the length of her own (it was, in fact, 34 lines of foolscap!). In her third letter to Jane, Anna clearly felt comfortable with her pen-friend. She said she would send a photo but warned, 'I'm ugly'. Obviously, this strategy functions as a premature apology and pre-empts a negative response.

By her fourth letter Anna felt confident enough to give Jane some gratuitous advice. Jane had detailed at length her birthday presents. Anna was clearly envious of her collection of presents and told Jane, 'you have very sincere relatives . . . I only got one (present) from my parents. So consider yourself lucky.' Interestingly, that comment was the kind Jane herself might have made in a similar context. It is probable that these very compatible writing partners intuitively recognized their shared outlook from even a few letters. There was little risk involved in Anna's comment and it was received benignly by Jane.

A move towards greater flexibility in writing characterized the early letters between the two girls. They both used interpolated comments, rhetorical questions, colloquialisms and exclamations which helped to make their writing interesting to a reader. Such language use was frequently present in the spoken language of both girls and was a natural part of their personality, together with their willingness to make personal disclosures. Anna led the way with her relaxed response to Jane's rather detached first letter, but Jane quickly responded in kind. Over time Jane became more effective in tempering her rhetorical flourishes according to her audience, whereas Anna was less discerning in their use, relying on them too heavily in inappropriate contexts such as her test letter to the principal (*Principal*).

Another interesting characteristic of the girls' early letter exchanges was the sustained awareness of each other as an interested audience. Anna was inclined to write at considerable length (one-and-a-half foolscap pages) detailing events of importance to her and interpolating comments on people and places. However, she acknowledged in the right places her audience's potential response. For example, after describing an accident on a bike and her injured finger, she wrote, 'Well that is enough on that eery subject. I was disappointed to see a short letter coming from you. As you usually write more.' (Anna's fifth letter to Jane.) It was Anna's accurate perception of a firm, personal relationship with Jane which gave her the confidence to make a gently negative comment about the length of Jane's letters.

Jane and Anna both enjoyed social talking and it is amusing to read Anna's concluding remark at the end of her seventh letter, 'Well guess that's all my head can think of but my mouth can say more when I want to, if you know what I mean.' The two writers were keen to talk on the phone but at my request they refrained from doing so. They shared an interest in drama and theatre activities which also provided a context for a shared problem. Jane wrote that she had gained a part in her Year 7 musical and would have to perform a solo. 'I know I can't do it! What on earth can I do? Another problem is none of my friends got in!!! What'll I do?' In the voice of experience Anna replied,

As for that problem of yours. I hope you'll go along with it. Because it's nothing. I volunteered to do a song in front of my school. Made a few booboos but that's how you get started. But I made it and won the Talent Quest. As for your friends well it all depends on the way they take it. If they sort of disliked you cause you made it don't worry they'll get over it, and once it's over they'll be even better friends than before. But if it isn't that way don't let me put ideas into your head. (I hope I don't sound bossy.). When I did a play Hansel and Gretel my friends were jealous. But eventually they were there when I had trouble. If they have a fight talk to them and prove that it wasn't your fault you made it and they didn't. You'll make it so don't worry. Remember, whatever you do, don't back out and once it's over you'll be much better.

Anna's interest in and strong empathy with Jane's acting problem was characteristic of her interest in her own social development, and in her testing of social reality. She was concerned to be popular with her peers but also aware of her need to be her own person. Even though Jane did not respond to Anna's well-meant advice, Anna did not seem to mind, suggesting that the process of writing out her feelings about various issues primarily served her own inner needs.

Anna initiated the next topic to be shared by the two writers: a discussion about famous people whom Anna would like to meet (the singer Olivia Newton-John and the tennis player Bjorn Borg). Anna then wrote about her own desire to be a famous singer and speculated that her future husband 'will probably get sick of the publicity (if I become famous)!'

Anna was not one to avoid reflection on real or imagined problems. She had a well-established practice of reflecting on experiences by the second year of the study and I thought she would have developed more noticeably in her test writing. As she wrote at the end of her seventh letter, 'Gee I can rave on or write about something once I get started.'

True as that was, Anna seemed to lack the concentration to revise or rewrite her work, and she failed to develop over time the judgement necessary to shape her expressive writing for a variety of purposes. Having discovered the pleasure of writing spontaneously for herself and close others, she was not prepared to forsake that to meet the demands of more exacting audiences.

Anna kept in touch with me long after the completion of the study. In the final year of her schooling she told me she was still having trouble anticipating the effects of her writing on distanced readers. Although her spontaneous writing in Year 7 was appropriate at that stage, she needed sustained, structured help to achieve the required differentiation of thought and language over time. Anna wrote in one of her letters 'I have this thing inside me that really urges me to write.' It is regrettable that her school experiences (including the writing intervention programme) did not provide her with more practice in authentic writing and greater exposure to good books. Anna's case highlights the need for sustained writing experiences across the curriculum, and informed feedback on the presence or absence of developmental characteristics.

Jane could have provided a model for Anna of structured and elaborated writing but the letter-writing mode alone and the nature of their relationship precluded that. Apart from exchanges about the relative lengths of their letters, both girls tended to stress their shared interests rather than any differences. The outstanding characteristic of their writing to each other was their amount of self-disclosure and the way they negotiated their relationship.

At one stage Anna's father was in and out of hospitals and she told Jane 'Mum cries. My younger brother and sister scream all day.' Jane's response to Anna's letter was to suggest she 'grin and bear it'. Heartless as that sounds, Jane continued: 'That is really hard, I know from experience. What you have to remember is that it can't go on forever.' She then recounted a problem she had

had with a friend while attending school in America. This was the first time Jane had openly shared with Anna her more personal life experiences. At this time I had shared with the writers a short story I had written and had published about a boy who had been rejected by his peers but finally won their respect. Jane commented in her letter to Anna:

> I think it's interesting that people take you how they see you on the outside. They don't think that you may be different inside. They take your outside looks and behaviour and make a character sketch of you without really knowing you inside.

Jane's was an accurate summary of the theme of the story. It is interesting to note that even though she might have been reflecting a personally felt response to the story, she managed to convey a sense of appropriate detachment in her generalization. Anna's comment on the story was more concrete: 'they end up believing he wasn't bad after all!'

Anna tried to continue the letter-writing exchange during the August vacation (Year 3 of the study) but discovered, when term started, that Jane had been to America for a holiday. Anna wrote: 'I was so thrilled to know my friend went to America . . . I can't wait till you tell me more. I am glad you had fun and to be honest I'm a little envious.'

Anna urged Jane to write at length about her experiences in America. She had identified so closely with Jane that any strongly envious feelings had been largely repressed as she recognized the possibility of enjoying vicariously Jane's travels. Typically for Anna, in the same letter, she anticipated the end of the intervention writing programme (fifteen months hence): 'I was wondering, when (we can't do) this writing thing . . . I won't hear of you as much . . . I mean writing all this time and being friends like this shouldn't go down the drain.'

Jane did write at considerable length about her American holiday. It would have been difficult to ignore Anna's real need for information and for confirmation that their pen-friendship was still viable. Anna experienced a sense of vulnerability in the relationship and was obviously anxious about its termination. She continued to sustain the writing exchange with spontaneous reflective letters about her personal life. She frequently addressed rhetorical questions to Jane, seeking similarities in their emotional responses, 'Do you cry? Do you get a sudden urge to keep a diary hoping one day after you have died that this diary will become famous and stumble across a fat, bald-headed film producer?'

Anna's sustained sense of humour belied her apparent problems. Jane remained relatively detached over this period. Then Anna met 'a wonderful guy'. That experience became a source of further letters to Jane and reflections upon the experience ('But I'm not desperate, I don't want to grow up too fast you know with guys and that.'). Anna's story about her meeting with Frank, the boyfriend, reveals her capacity to write with unconscious irony, honesty and freshness:

> Occasionally he'd give me the eye. Occasionally I did . . . at one stage we had a short straight conversation . . . and it was the first time I ever felt the way I felt with this guy . . . at the end of the day I waved to him and he gave the most beautiful smile. And to

be honest I think I've forgotten what he looked like. I've got to be alone in a quiet area and concentrate hard to remember.

The engaging quality of this account attests to the intrinsic appeal of authentic writing.

While Anna's enthusiasm for the relationship with Jane was consistent, Jane had periods of ambivalence during which her letters were brief, with apologies. However, on her return from America she felt she had something interesting to write about and she sent Anna several lengthy, detailed accounts of her trip. Interestingly, she referred back to Anna's interest in writing a book: 'You know what you said about the book you wanted to write or the diary. Well, I don't think this at all funny or moronic because when I was reading it I was really shocked because that's just what I've always thought, too.'

A lengthy account followed of Jane's conflicted experiences with her mother and of her need to write out those experiences, influenced by *The Diary of Anne Frank*. Jane was still worried about the possibilities of her personal diary writing being discovered by an unsympathetic reader. Anna's wish for a relationship with Jane based on shared perceptions was confirmed by Jane's disclosures. Anna wrote:

Gee that was really something discovering that you feel the same way about the book. You don't feel so silly if someone thinks the same as me in certain ways. . . . You see sometimes I'm afraid to give an opinion because I'm afraid I'll be laughed at.

Anna then asked Jane to her school dance. Anna was very anxious at this time to meet Jane in person. It was measure of Jane's social maturity that she declined the invitation with honesty and social grace:

I find it easier to write things to you than say them. You see, you asked me to the school dance and well I've never been to anything like that before and I wouldn't know how to tell my mother and I just don't think I would enjoy it seeing that it would be the first one I've been to and I wouldn't know anyone. I hope you don't think I'm a little sop or anything. And thank you very much but I just don't think it would work out.

Jane then referred again to Anna's interest in writing about her problems: 'when I get really cross or frustrated or upset I write down everything and it really helps.' Possibly Jane sensed she might be alienating Anna with her non-acceptance of the dance invitation so she found a shared concern to draw attention again to their friendship.

Early in the final year of the study Anna reprimanded Jane for not replying to her letters, reminding her of the efforts she, Anna, had made to keep in touch: 'The least you could do for me is write a good long letter back . . . I hope this won't get you as cranky as I am now . . . P.S. I am very annoyed.'

Anna's annoyance was reasonable. Jane did reply with a lengthy letter with excuses, some strong self-justifications and an apology. Anna replied '. . . let's clear the air . . . you couldn't blame me for getting annoyed but since I showed how angry I was I find it only fair to say sorry. But then again you had your share of telling (me) off as well.' Later in the same letter she wrote, '. . . do you think I look nice in these photos. I do look a bit weird. I don't know if you read the letter where I mentioned you look good too.'

It is interesting how effectively Anna and Jane maintained a balance in their relationship, resolving conflicts through writing and by endorsing each other's self-esteem at appropriate times. Such is the nature of peer relationships that these writers could use social forms of writing which would be inappropriate in the context of writing to a teacher; even a teacher regarded as a close other. As well, this experience provided Jane and Anna with an opportunity to test the effectiveness of their written confrontations, the success of which (like their relationship) depended upon their perceptive judgements and sensitive language choices. Clearly most school writing does not provide a suitable range of contexts in which students can experiment realistically with socially relevant written-language forms.

Since writing was the source of the girls' relationship, it was fitting that Jane began to reflect in her letters to Anna on her own writing practices. She was very busy with rehearsals for a musical and she regretted the lack of opportunity to concentrate on her writing. She perceived the need to become involved with characters and plot in order to write a good story and she thought it was easier to write stories when she was younger: 'I have better and more complex ideas now but I never seem to actually sit and write them.'

It is a reality of secondary-school life that there is little time to write at length and with sustained reflection, particularly with the fragmentation of school timetables and competing extra-curricular events.

As I mentioned earlier, towards the end of the study I asked the writers to write a letter as an interested applicant in reply to a fictitious advertisement for exchange students from this country. The follow-up task was to write a reply from the family accepting the application, and finally a letter supposedly written while living as that exchange student. The purpose of the tasks was to encourage the writers to decentre and to write from different points of view. It was interesting to compare Anna's and Jane's letters of application. Jane wrote an efficient, suitably detailed, detached but effective letter of application. Anna wrote a longer, messier, informative but more personal application. The reader of Jane's letter would not have been able to fault her writing but would have had minimal information about her personality. Anna provided more insight into her person-ality with her rhetorical asides and her expressed enthusiasm for the proposed exchange. While both girls would have been similarly attractive as exchange students to a host family, Anna's family would have gained a clearer sense of the kind of person she was from the expressiveness of her letter than they would have had of Jane from her writing. Jane, however, in her test writing showed a greater range of language options and more fitting sense of judgement in her discourse choices.

Anna and Jane continued their letters to the end of the final year of the study but they also shared their more structured writing, such as sustained arguments or comments on aspects of life from different points of view. By now, Jane's written language showed a consistent ability to structure embedded sentences and to use cohesive devices. She could put forward propositions, explore their consequences, then reflect on the personal experiences which were influencing her point of view.

In a fictional account of a day in the life of a restaurant manager, Anna showed she could identify with characters and write from their perspective. Strong as her identification was, there was still a short-coming in her writing in the over-use of colloquial language and a tendency to switch focus too abruptly in one paragraph.

The relationship between Anna and Jane was particularly interesting for me to observe because I knew how similar they were in temperament and personality. The difference in degree of personal involvement in the relationship, with Anna clearly investing more energy in it, is probably accounted for by the differences in their family and social life. Anna was inclined to live life more vicariously than Jane, through television, reading and daydreaming. Both girls read keenly but Anna read more romantic novels and less non-fiction than Jane. Jane had more real-life experiences in overseas travel and varieties of entertainment than Anna. Jane had learnt to contain much of her inner psychic energy (once her excessive talking was modified), while Anna expressed hers wherever there was an opportunity. Jane had a better developed sense of judgement in terms of what to express and what to repress. As well, she had well-developed capacities to structure her thought and language in a variety of ways according to context. Both girls were personally appealing for their high energy levels and for their ready enthusiasm for life and experiences. They did meet after the study finished and, according to Anna, the meeting was a success.

Conclusion

What does this analysis of the relationship between Anna and Jane, established and maintained through writing, reveal about the process of developing writing abilities? Clearly, for Anna, her need for a peer audience and Jane's meeting of that need were a powerful motivator in the continuation of her writing and its amount. Although her lengthy letters to Jane (usually one-and-a-half foolscap pages) were fairly self-involved, she knew how to hold Jane's interest by interpolating rhetorical questions and/or by endorsing her self-esteem with appropriate comments. Perhaps the letter-writing exchange was more self-enhancing for Anna than it was cognitively or linguistically developing. The essential differences between the writers were apparent in Jane's greater language flexibility and consistent rhetorical sophistication. They shared similar imaginative capacities, though Anna's scores for Creativity were higher than Jane's.

Anna's eventual willingness to write more freely and more spontaneously than Jane probably allowed her to demonstrate more effectively her creative potential.

On her overall scores she did not demonstrate development as markedly as Jane because she was not as skilled in connecting and synthesizing her ideas. Nor was she much concerned with using punctuation or paragraphs. Anna had little trouble writing at length even in her test writing, nor did she seem to experience difficulties in writing authentically for an examining audience: the same relaxed tone is consistently evident in both her intervention and her test writing. Anna's difficulties lay in ordering her thoughts and balancing her personal needs in writing with the demands in some contexts for formal, structured writing. On some occasions Anna redrafted her writing in the intervention programme but it was a pity there was not more time or opportunity to help Anna with this developmental necessity. She was the kind of writer whose ability could have been enhanced by consistent work on the editing process, although she might have lost some of her interest in writing, had she been required to rework it. Her large, immature and sometimes illegible handwriting deteriorated over the time of the study while Jane's was neat, easy to read and efficient-looking. Minimal as this influence may be on a reader, it can create negative effects on an impatient reader.

Summary

- The relationship between Jane and Anna was one of the most interesting in the study. It was a relationship tested by the usual fluctuations in degree of commitment and temporary ambivalences (particularly for Jane). It was interesting that the relationship continued so strongly in spite of some difficulties and the temporary breaks over school holidays and during examination periods. Anna was able to confront Jane effectively. Jane was able to recognize Anna's commitment to the relationship, even though her enthusiasm for it was not as high.
- The partners' mutual ability to establish and maintain a written dialogue attests to the tacit relating abilities they were able to communicate through their writing. The challenge now is to consider how we might best harness and develop those abilities within school contexts.

Postscript

As I was finishing this book Anna rang me. We have kept in touch over the years. I asked her how she saw the writing project on reflection now. She said it gave her an opportunity to write in depth, to express what she had inside and it developed her initiative for writing: 'I'm still into it (writing) . . . prior to my wedding day I wrote my husband a poem about our meeting, and I've written my grandmother a letter telling her what she means to me . . . I'm too shy to show it to her yet.'

She also spoke about the value of Jane to her as an audience and writing partner because she could idealize her acceptance of her.

I felt older, wiser, and a bit sentimental when we finished talking.

6 Simon: a writer with potential

I have chosen Simon to discuss here because, although he showed only slight development in his test writing over the four years, he gave me some important insights into his writing processes and his thinking. I felt there was more to him than was revealed by his quiet manner.

In his early interviews with me in Year 6, Simon was fairly restrained but also reflective and thoughtful about his approaches to writing. He thought it would be helpful to have someone to discuss his ideas with before he began writing as he had trouble thinking up ideas. I suggested he keep a journal but he did not think that would help much; he needed someone beside him to motivate his writing.

It emerged that Simon was very interested in the breeding and caring of birds and this interest was a theme of his conversations and his writing. He liked writing stories for his father because 'he likes birds . . . he understands me as well', but 'Mum rouses at you if you get a mistake. Dad advises you.' Simon found it hard to write for his teacher as he was usually 'a bit on edge', wondering what the teacher would say. In Simon's mind, writing involved keeping a wary eye and an alert ear on the intended audience.

An incident occurred in the school early in the first year of the study where a group of Simon's classmates brutally killed some chickens and injured others, 'for fun'. Simon was upset by the incident and took home one of the injured chickens to care for it. He spoke to me at some length about his anger and sadness, and he was keen at first to write more about his feelings and reactions in a journal. However, next time I saw him he said he had had too much homework to write a journal. Had journal writing been a routine class activity it might have served a special purpose in helping Simon come to terms with an upsetting experience.

I discussed with Simon the differences between writing down the teacher's notes from the blackboard and using one's own language. Simon remarked that it was harder to use one's own words but he thought you learn more by doing so. Simon gave me the impression that he was more reflective about himself and the world around him than he was prepared to talk about. He needed to feel secure to reveal his thoughts and feelings. He was more responsive to me after I had told him of my own experiences of keeping birds as a child.

In his sentence completion task at the end of the first year of the study, Simon wrote, 'I feel I'm in trouble', in response to the prompt, 'When I am asked to write in school . . .' No wonder he liked writing best when 'I do it on my own.'

In the first of the concentration and free-association pieces Simon wrote fairly cursorily, listing little more than a catalogue of sights and sounds around him. He made the comment 'it is easy to write down my thoughts but hard to think of them.' Simon needed consistent help in focusing his inner speech for some purpose. The letter-writing exchange gave Simon's writing new life. He became quite self-revealing to his writing partner Juliet, whom, of course he had never met. I am reminded of Anna's comment that it helped in some ways to know you did not have to meet your writing partner face to face. Juliet was an unselfconscious writer with a confident, nonchalant personality which Simon found encouraging. Juliet revealed enough about herself in the initial letter of the exchange for Simon to feel interested in writing back. After writing his address in the body of his first letter (to ensure Juliet's reply – he had forgotten that I was acting as courier), he apologized for his untidy writing and then detailed some of his likes and dislikes about school. He then moved into more personally revealing information: 'At school I often get into trouble for almost all ranges of bad habits. Except that I don't smoke.'

In his self-presentation Simon took some risks but he was able to focus his inner speech on a dialogue with an imagined other. He assumed correctly that Juliet would want to hear his reactions to school and something about his interests and personality. Although he did not elaborate any of his points in much detail, for an initial letter of introduction he managed to balance well the need to reveal some aspects of self with an awareness of the interest level of his reading audience.

In her second letter Juliet provided Simon with a model for a longer, more elaborated letter when she wrote partly in point form, listing and commenting on a number of aspects of her life. (There were twenty-one points in her letter.) Simon decided to copy her model for his reply, acknowledging the help she had unwittingly given him: 'I like the way you set out your letter so I think I'll do the same.' With this endorsement of Juliet, and with his self-revelations, Simon was able to establish rapport with Juliet. As time went on, he became more confident in expressing his self-doubts and his feelings about the letters they exchanged. He liked receiving long letters from Juliet but it worried him that there was an implicit expectation that he reply in as much length: 'Please don't make the letter too long because I have to write as well as read them (and time is short).'

Simon was very conscious of matching himself against Juliet, not in a competitive way but as a way of showing empathy with her expectations and feelings. In reacting to the points she had listed in her letter, he noted the similarities in their likes and dislikes, and any shared feelings. In response to Juliet's comments about her friends, Simon wrote 'I probably have about the same amount of friends as you. But they are only friends sometimes and the rest of the time, I can tell you, I don't need enemy's.'

Juliet had asked Simon how many children he wanted to have and he replied quite frankly 'I haven't really thought about children much so I have no idea how many I want.' Simon finished his letter with a plea, 'I repeat please do not write more next letter unless it's imperative.' When Juliet wrote a postscript to her letter, 'P.S. I am a shrimp.' , Simon wrote in reply, 'Size doesn't mean a thing.' These writing partners were unconsciously negotiating the terms of their relationship and acknowledging their sensitivity to each other. The tact and skill involved in this are impressive and all too often not called for in most school writing.

Although Juliet was a more able and confident writer than Simon, he was able to respond to the sub-texts of her writing and his self-reflectiveness and sensitivity became a spring for the developing relationship between them. Simon probably needed Juliet more than she needed him as a motivating audience for his writing. In his third letter to Juliet he wrote 'I agree that we probably will no[know] a fair bit about each other and also that it is hard writing to someone I don't know. It is a bit easier now that I have your letter to refer to.'

Simon had an intuitive ability to create a sense of relationship between himself and Juliet by picking up her comments and adding an endorsing comment of his own. For example: 'I enjoy holidays very much and share your enthusiasm . . . we also have a pool and it sounds like my dad is like yours, too lazy to clean it. . . . I am dying to meet you and hope she [the author] can arrange it.'

Simon's ability to create a sense of empathy with Juliet through his intuitive understanding of human relationships and his good sense in using her writing as a source for ideas are worth noting because they reflect some of the complex of abilities which influence writing development.

I think that Simon's unconscious motive in letting Juliet know that her letters mattered to him was to ensure a reply to his own. Such is the recursiveness of the process that this in turn would endorse his sense of self-worth and his capacity to communicate effectively.

Although Simon's language was appropriate in register and cohesiveness, he was still experimenting in his early letters to Juliet with the kinds of thoughts and feelings he might comfortably reveal in his letters. In his choice of format and subject matter he tended to be guided by her letters to him. As it happened, she was very self-revealing and unselfconscious in her writing. This seemed to liberate Simon more than his earlier school writing experiences had done. Simon now had a focus for his inner speech and he was keen to meet Juliet's unstated expectations of him as a writer. This created some ambivalence in him. In his fifth letter he started, 'I am glad your letter is shorter and I hope you keep with this.' However, further down the page he wrote 'Your letter could be a little bigger like a page or two and I won't mind but please don't write 4 pages until we've written about 10 letters and get to know each other a bit better. I can't keep up.'

The imagined closeness of Juliet as an interested reader of his letters helped

Simon produce more writing than he did in class. His letter writing was close in form to written-down speech, though there was less back-tracking, and fewer incomplete sentences than in speech. He used comments, asides, rhetorical questions, jokes, anecdotes and responses to Juliet's comments as part of his discourse range, much the same as one does in a conversation with a friend. But rarely as one does in writing to a teacher.

When the students were looking for subjects to write about in their letters I suggested they could write about writing. In his letter to Juliet, Simon wrote,

> I find it difficult to start off writing without a lead. That is one reason I like getting your letters . . . I like reading a lot and I think it helps a lot with my writing . . . I am beginning to enjoy writing more and more and I think it is because I'm reading more and more. I like writing these letters especially to you. These classes probably help me to write better but most of the magic is in the brain. I think I'm fairly good at writing.

Simon's poetic insight that most of the magic is in the brain was a spontaneous flash of creativity which justifies the theoretical importance of reflective, self-expressive writing. He recognized unconsciously that the ability to write effectively was inherent in himself, stimulated by his reading and a conducive environment.

An interesting movement in thought was evident in Simon's next letter to Juliet. He was reassuring Juliet about what she considered was her untidy handwriting. (Many students correlate good writing abilities with good hand-writing abilities.) He wrote 'Don't think you write untidy cause I don't think I write too neatly . . . Compared to your friends writing your's is very neat. I can read it at least.'

Simon encouraged and mirrored Juliet by making comparisons between his handwriting and hers. He then progressed in thought from a measure of egocentricity to a more universal reference: the (hand)writing's legibility. In embryonic form this is the kind of movement in thought which occurs through the development of discourse and can be seen in even fleeting ways within parts of the writing of developing writers.

Simon then went on to recount the story of his being 'busted at school for stealing starter units out of the heaters.' He wrote as if the practice were something like an infection, 'I expect its been through your school but in case it hasn't I'll tell you about it.' He gave the impression that his own involvement was something for which he felt no responsibility or regret until he 'got caught' and had to pay twenty dollars for a new unit. It is interesting that Simon's well-developed sensitivity to the welfare of birds was not paralleled in his general moral/ethical development. His close experiences with birds probably account for his concern for them, while his capacity to think about people and issues in the abstract was still fairly egocentric – albeit his sensitivity to Juliet's opinion of him.

In Simon's expressive writing the factor influencing his choices seemed to be his awareness of Juliet as an audience. His writing was self-revealing and often disparate. His apparently random connections between items of information, thoughts and feelings were dictated by a logic arising from his developing awareness of himself in relation to another. He assumed that Juliet could follow his logic. By juxtaposing his references to Juliet's handwriting with his story about his own vandalizing activities he revealed that assumption, as well as his yet undifferentiated sense of the incongruity of that juxtaposition.

The formulating principle for Simon's writing at this point seemed to be to reflect himself to another, with a surprising lack of conscious concern about the kinds of judgement Juliet might have made about his behaviour. That is, Simon could empathetically reassure Juliet about her handwriting which was the medium for their relationship, yet he showed no awareness of her possible disapproval of his stealing. He felt no guilt apparently, and the activities were peripheral to their relationship except as part of the developing self-revelations of their letter exchange.

At an unconscious level Simon could have been feeling some discomfort about the starter-lighter incident and using Juliet as a mirror for some implicit evaluation of his experiences: would she see him as bad or brave? Whatever the motivation it is conducive to development as a writer and thinker that mistakes in both language and judgement can be made, and retrieved, without undue threat to the enabling relationship. This freedom was implicit in Simon and Juliet's relationship.

At this point in his development as a writer and thinker, Simon was operating at a fairly intuitive level. His self-awareness was becoming more consciously differentiated through his relationship with Juliet who provided valuable, though non-specific, feedback. When Simon expressed to Juliet his difficulty in writing a long story at home, he revealed his need for both an audience other than self to sustain his writing, as well as his need for a perceptible audience – an audience whose sense he had sufficiently internalized to be able to envisage. The fact that he mentioned this difficulty to Juliet suggests that he was exploring the issue unconsciously but with her in mind.

I think all this points to the complex nature of the role of audience in writing. If you think back to the theoretical arguments I presented for the spiral model for writing development it incorporates the interrelatedness of self and others in writing development. Implicitly, a sense of self and others is variously significant for different kinds of writing experiences. An empathetic relationship with another as audience can often create different kinds of language, imagery and content which serve both conscious and unconscious purposes for the writer. Just as that language, imagery and content may serve different purposes for the reader. Hence my difficulty with the genre approach to writing development which fails to take account of the differing purposes a piece of writing might serve for the writer and the reader.

In Simon's case we can discern different levels of his self-development even within one letter. His awareness of his need for a close other as audience was finely developed as we can see in his endorsements of Juliet, yet his sense of social ethics was at a relatively undifferentiated stage (the starter-lighters incident). He wants approval for his social skills of relating sensitively to another, but he seems indifferent to approval or disapproval for anti-social behaviour. From the writing alone one can only surmise that this indifference was genuine, and not bravado.

I think these comments reflect some of the complexities we encounter when we try to assess a student's writing development. When we formulate writing experiences which help students to reflect themselves and to develop themselves as individuals, we have to take account of the cognitive, affective, ethical and social aspects of the writer's self which naturally emerge from such tasks. Linguistic analyses alone are insufficient to take account of the complex nature of writing. For example, the writer's main purpose for writing can influence the choice of content and structure and even in the course of writing the purpose can change. Once we start to analyse Simon's writing in cognitive, affective, social and linguistic terms we can see discrepancies in stages of development, even within the one piece. Different contexts and audiences can influence different kinds of development and writing programmes need to take into account the range of functions and purposes which writing can serve, far beyond those tested solely by linguistic analyses, important as they are. In Simon's letter writing his appropriate sense of audience and purpose was a consistent factor. Against this consistency, his developing sense of self was revealed with both progressions and regressions as he struggled to make sense of, for example, himself and his school experiences.

The more you look closely at a body of work from one writer, the more aware you become of the complexity of writing processes and products. Generalized assessment schemas can provide a framework for comparative and even individual assessments, but much of significance is lost in the generalization.

Simon's history as a writer prompts me to ask 'What can writing do for the writer?' I think from Simon's case, and the other case studies, we can infer mental processes which seem to serve some integrating needs for the writer, such as seeing one's thoughts reflected back to oneself and being positively mirrored by an audience. In Simon's case his sense of audience in his letter writing was well developed and well internalized, but other less well-developed aspects of his thinking needed to emerge for conscious, or even unconscious, exploration, integration and further development. Hence the value of providing contexts which motivate students to continue writing.

If nothing more happens in the process of composing than that writers become more self-aware and enhanced by the anticipation of a positively mirroring audience, then at least they have experienced themselves as able to symbolize themselves and their experiences. It may be a romantic fantasy but early cave drawings may attest to this concept.

Simon's reference to the magic in the brain is an example of one writer's metaphoric integration of his inner and outer world. It is also a humbling reminder that a teacher can do most when he or she connect writers to their own inner magic. In our teaching role we do not create the magic – only the enabling context, the audience to clap the writer and the wizardry to work with the magic when it appears. If only it could all be done with the wave of a wand!

In the second year of the letter-writing exchange there was a noticeable increase in confidence in Simon's rhetoric. He could start his letters with chatty comments which helped Juliet to centre on his frame of mind and helped him to enter into the spirit of his letter to her. This technique occurs naturally in relaxed conversation, but it often has to be recognized as appropriate in personal letter writing. Simon was an inhibited writer at the beginning of my work with him, but he was responsive to encouragement from Juliet and me to be himself in writing. When he wrote naturally and easily, Simon's reflective thinking became more apparent.

In a free-association piece written at the beginning of the third year of the study, Simon wrote 'I have been thinking about what I'm going to do over the next few years. When I'll die and so on. I wonder what's going on at home but mainly I'm thinking this page that I'm writing now.' Simon was aware that Juliet was a more accomplished writer than he: 'I wish my writing had improved as much as yours . . . I wish you had written more . . . It would have made it easier for me.'

But he saw Juliet as a collaborative partner rather than a competitive one and he enjoyed sharing his thoughts with her. His newsy letters were often interspersed with reflective comments such as: 'Yesterday as you might know the world was supposed to end. If you know who profecised [sic] this for sure please tell me. I am quite interested.'

Simon was reluctant to write compositions in his regular English classes; 'Most of the time I am asked to write a composition I get a bad response, mainly because I don't do the writing.'

In some respects Simon was defensive in his relationships with others. He seemed popular with his peers but often appeared distanced from them. He liked very few teachers and, predictably, he rejoiced in misbehaving in school. A poignant sense of loneliness came through in a project he wrote on animals: 'I like animals because some can cuddle you and if their well brought up you can do this often to while away the time.' He explained that his father liked birds best and his mother liked cats: 'I guess this is why I like them both best.'

Simon was not an eager conversationalist and I learnt most about him from his writing. Without that source of evidence of his thinking and feeling capacity it would have been easy to regard him as an uninterested and withdrawn student. It was his slightly provocative streak in his manner and his shy defensiveness which suggested to me that there might be more going on in his mind than he would readily reveal. In that sense, then, his letters were a revelation. He was quietly pleased when I commented on his 'magic in the brain' remark. He wrote to Juliet about my response and said he did not remember writing the comment. His defensiveness broke down when one of his class mates, enthusiastic Anna, said she thought it was 'a great remark' and proceeded to write her own story in response to it. Simon blushed and went on with his own writing.

In the final year of the study both Juliet and Simon became interested in writing stories for a general audience so their letters to each other were less frequent. Each berated the other for not writing more often, even though they shared the stories they wrote. Simon enjoyed story writing now as a kind of escapism (he had been in trouble for shoplifting). In one story, 'Another school', he described very vividly a dreamlike sequence where he was attacked by an unknown force and found himself in future time. Although the theme of the story was familiar enough, Simon's sense of drama and pace created a powerfully evocative sense of the experience of disassociation. Unfortunately, or ironically, he did not finish the story. Considering the high level of concentration obvious to me while he was writing it, it might have been hard for him to maintain the initial sense of urgency which prompted his imagination.

Simon's test writing

Simon's test-writing scores showed some slight development, with regressions, over the four-year period. Of more interest, however, was the content of his test writing. Even in his first test piece (*Space*) his reflective thinking was apparent: 'It is easy to write about something when we know about a subject. I shouldn't say that because sometimes its the other way round. Sometimes its easier to use our imagination.'

In his letter outlining his response to the extract from *Kes* the predominant feature of Simon's account was his identification with the victims in the story. He thought the headmaster should have guessed that the messenger boy had nothing to do with the smoking incident, 'but being caught with the goods is just as bad as being caught in the act.' He felt that Billy Casper 'could have probably stayed awake if he really tried but all assemblies are kinda boring and I'v almost gone to sleep sometimes myself.' Had Simon been able to sustain and elaborate his reflections on the incident, he might have scored higher than 10.5 (out of 20) on his test.

Interestingly, he addressed his test writing to Juliet. It could be that he mistakenly saw no necessity to give her full details of the incident or an elaborated account of his reactions. He was used to making free-ranging comments in his regular letters to her. In fact, the extent of his detail about *Kes* was greater than he usually devoted to any one incident in his letters. Interestingly, he did try to deal with the complex moral issues involved in the extract:

> I don't believe that Macdowell should have got the cane for coughing, but it must have been a tough school. Then again if he was doing it on purpose I guess he deserved something but still two strokes are a bit rough.

In his test letter to the *Principal* (written in the final year of the study) Simon wrote about a number of good ideas for improving the school and elaborated quite effectively on the value of these ideas. Although he only scored 13 out of 20 (the averaged marks of two markers) he seemed to have put considerable effort into thinking out his ideas. Unfortunately he lacked some of the finer points of rhetoric appropriate for a letter to a school principal. He did not finish his test paper and there was evidence of great haste apparent in his handwriting. Simon usually took a long time to think out his stories and letters and he hated having to rush his writing. His letter to the principal lacked the zest and personality often apparent in his spontaneous writing, but that may not be surprising in view of Simon's experiences with school authorities.

Simon's *Future* piece written at the end of the study was imaginative, though less detailed than his earlier fantasies. He did say that what he would most like to do is 'live out the life of a science fiction character.'

The person who emerged from the test pieces in the study was not as interesting or complex as the person I came to know over the four years of the intervention programme. Although this is not surprising, it does suggest some of the limitations of drawing profiles of writers solely from test writing. It also suggests some of the limitations of writing done in classrooms where the teacher is the sole audience.

Possibly Simon's early test piece (*Space*) scored well in Year 6 (13 out of 20) because he still had some sense of an examining teacher as a sympathetic reader. Certainly he sounded less confident and more restrained in his letter test pieces than in any other writing done in the intervention programme. While it is difficult to attribute Simon's lack of clear development in writing (he scored 13, 10, 10.5, 13, 14.5 out of 20 for *Space*, *Peer*, *Kes*, *Principal* and *Future* respectively) to the pressure of test conditions, it would have been interesting to see whether Simon could have been helped with more specific work on understanding and meeting the demands of test writing. It is a bit hard to imagine his seeing that as a very useful purpose for writing.

Summary

- What emerged over the four years of the study was a picture of a writer with complex responses to social situations: a writer with deep sensitivities only revealed in very comfortable, non-threatening contexts: an imaginative thinker with an interest in his own place in the world, but one cautious about discussing his ideas and feelings too openly. I suspect that Simon would have become more closed as the demands of senior school work became apparent to him. He was not an avid reader (though he thought he read a lot) and he talked little at school, though he was a reflective thinker.
- Simon found the natural world an interesting place. He did not write engagingly in test conditions, nor did he write well in haste. Like many sensitive and potentially able writers, Simon needed more time to write than he or his teachers realized. He also needed a particularly patient and empathetic reader/audience to provide a mirroring, endorsing source of stimulation for his writing, thinking and feeling.
- Writers like Simon often create a false impression of independence, unlike

Anna who was very aware of her need for support and self-mirroring. I often wonder whether the magic in Simon's brain conjured up new marvels for him through his continued imaginative writing, or whether the birds and animals he loved had to provide solace, stimulation and self-endorsement.

7 Anton and John: less able writers

I have chosen these two writers to discuss in some detail because they are the kind of students who most often frustrate us, not necessarily because of their shortcomings but often because school systems do not allow us to provide the intensive, flexible and individual work students need. Anton in the middle of the writing-ability range and John towards the end of it may remind you of many students you know. Both were quiet and unobtrusive in class, yet you would not completely overlook them. Where John showed no motivation to change, Anton was very conscientious. Persistent presence you cannot ignore. These characters are usually given minor roles in a good story but, as they represent a reality we know well, I'll see what I can do with them. In spite of my slightly disparaging tone here, I liked both students, partly because they seemed appreciative of any attention, however slight.

Anton

Anton came from a Greek family. His parents had emigrated to Australia as children. His father was a cabinet maker and his mother was an office clerk. Anton was rather shy but we gradually developed a comfortable relationship and I gradually realized he liked writing, especially for the pleasure of seeing his ideas committed to paper. This pleasure increased noticeably when he started writing to Sally, his writing partner.

Anton was the kind of student you overlook at first but over a period of time his personable qualities, the consistency in his writing methods and his steady reflectiveness attracted my attention. Slowly, and largely unconsciously, he drew attention to himself by retaining a sense of his own person, often against the prevailing class mood. Anton rarely expressed difficulties with writing and he managed to complete tasks with a minimum of fuss. On reflection I think this was more because he did not want to be a bother than a mark of his confidence. It was not until the end of the second year of the study that I really began to take a particular interest in the content of Anton's writing.

Anton was able to present himself in an interesting way to Sally. He revealed a maturity in establishing his relationship with her which I had not noticed earlier. In the realistic social situation of writing to a peer Anton could tap tacit powers of expression which had not been evident, understandably, in his earlier interviews with me. He wrote with enthusiasm to Sally and at the end of the study nominated his letters to her as the most interesting writing he had done during the previous three years.

Simultaneously with writing his letters to Sally, Anton continued his interest in narrative writing. He showed me a letter he had written for history in which he imagined himself as a new settler in early Australia. His own family background as migrants must have made the task particularly relevant. He clearly enjoyed identifying with historical characters and immersed himself in the atmosphere of the period. His involvement rather contradicted his admission to Sally, 'I don't have much feelings.'

When, to provide some variety in the writing programme I asked the writers to write about a world in which everything were edible, Anton responded with great enthusiasm. There was a lively discussion in the group for about twenty minutes prior to writing and Anton decided to write about an edible soccer field. He even returned to his classroom at lunchtime to finish his 'edible story'. Clearly the imaginative nature of the task enthused him – as did the foolproof combination of food and games, I'm sure.

Anton wrote in the sentence-completion tasks I set to gather data on the writers' attitudes to writing that coming to the writing sessions was the best help he could get with his writing. He said he now enjoyed writing and had written more stories than normal. It was rather surprising that Anton felt the sessions made a difference as he rarely asked for specific help and gave the impression he did not need it. He knew I liked his 'edible story' and I made occasional comments to him about his letters to Sally. I think it was sufficient motivation for him to feel valued as a writer just by engaging in pleasurable, meaningful writing tasks. For him, the primary function of the writing group was to provide a context which would enhance his identity as a writer. Undoubtedly Anton's relationship with Sally was important to him. I guess for a shy boy it can be helpful to relate to a girl through letter writing, particularly when you like writing anyway. It was typical of Anton's self-effacing manner that at the beginning of the third year of the study (by which time he had written seven letters to Sally) he started his first letter of that year with, 'I don't know if you remember me from last year. I am Anton.'

Sally was, in fact, a difficult writing partner for Anton. She had a quick, sharp manner and could be quite scornful in her group about Anton's letters to her, especially when he wrote at length about soccer. She was exasperated with his preoccupations and very astute in her judgements about his personality and abilities. She was intellectually more mature than Anton and she knew it. She rarely put effort into her letters to him as she did not care much about him. Sally always took a provocative point of view in any discussion and she enjoyed verbal sparring with her peers and with me. She could easily intimidate other students, though she could also be deflated herself by teachers and adults. In essence, she was not fully aware of her alienating effect upon others, or of the abrasiveness of many of her remarks. None of this came through in her letters to Anton, so he had no reason to see Sally as other than interested in him as a peer writing partner. He tolerated her almost illegible handwriting until she stated in one letter to him her wish to become a journalist. He replied 'Some good advice. If you want to be a journalist you will have to learn how to write neater.' Needless to say, Sally was infuriated by his remark.

It is interesting to speculate that a relationship which functioned quite adequately through letter-writing might have been less successful had the partners met personally. For Anton, the fantasy or image of an interested audience for his writing was sufficient in itself. Sally rarely made any effort to endorse Anton's ego, yet he continued to see her in a positive way. It is perhaps significant that the issue of 'an image' is mentioned here – Anton was very anxious to see what Sally looked like and asked for her photo several times. Eventually he did see her photo but passed no comment. Perhaps he just needed some concrete image of her. She certainly did not reveal much of her self in writing to Anton and I felt sorry for Anton in the mismatch between them as writing partners. He deserved better.

Anton's strengths as a writer were his readiness to engage himself in the process of writing, his ability to identify with the needs of his audience and to provide sufficient details in writing to create an impression of his subject. By his seventh letter to Sally, Anton had adopted a conversational tone which marked his increased confidence. His earlier letters had been rather stilted and predictable. Now he could outline at the beginning of the letter what he wanted to write about and engage his reader's interest. Like Simon, Anton revealed more about his experiences and fantasies in his writing than would ever have been expected from his conversations in the writing group.

It is worth considering what the survey of writing done over a two-week period in Year 9 revealed in Anton's case. His tally of total lines in all subjects written in that time showed that more than half his writing was set by the teachers and involved copying from the blackboard, or from a book. Over the two weeks of the survey, Anton wrote 1,007 lines of writing (across the curriculum) of which 610 lines were set by the teachers as copy work. In addition, teachers set a total of 229 lines where Anton used his own words. Anton set himself 147 lines of writing (25 lines in English, 112 lines in history and 10 lines in maths). The self-set history essay was unusual but Anton enjoyed the subject and liked writing imaginative essays. If it were not for Anton's initiative in setting himself an essay in history, most of his writing over the two-week period of the survey would have involved copy writing. No wonder he enjoyed writing in the intervention group.

Anton's test writing

Anton's test-writing scores did show significant development over the four-year period. Interestingly, when I looked closely at his test writing, I could 'hear' the same stilted tone of voice as that of his early letters to Sally. In his sentence-completion tasks, Anton had said that, when writing for a test, he tried to do his best. Given the amount of informative/copy writing which Anton did in class, it is possible that he perceived test writing as requiring a concentration upon informative writing. To Anton, that meant keeping to facts and not offering any risky expressiveness.

Anton's letter to the principal, towards the end of the writing programme, was lengthier than his other test pieces and more elaborated, scoring an average of 11 out of a possible 20. At the end of that letter he made a personal and expressive plea to the principal – an expression of personality absent from his other test letters. Perhaps now he felt more comfortable about his writing – a worthwhile development since Year 6 (in his *Space* letter) when his major concern was for neatness and correctness in writing:

> All people here in Australia where I live and go to school always are taught to write neatly and on the lines, which are meant to be on paper. We are also taught to write without making mistakes, this is called spelling.

In the total test population Anton was an average writer. He was very anxious to conform to teachers' expectations, and mine I expect. Had he had more confidence in writing authentically and expressively in his test writing, Anton might have demonstrated more development over the four years. Certainly it would have helped had he had more expressive and imaginative writing experiences across the curriculum. Many students, like Anton, must perceive that to be other-than-themselves in writing is often more effective in assessment tasks than to express their own writing voice. Anton had found his writing voice in his letters to Sally, and in his imaginative stories. But he stilled it in his test writing with the result that he appeared less able to differentiate his thought and language than he was in non-test writing. To me, Anton's test writing sounded truncated, and split from his expressiveness.

Needless to say, unless a concept of writing development can effectively synthesize both the individual and universal characteristics inherent in its nature, both in curriculum practices and in testing procedures, potentially able writers like Anton may fail for obeying the wrong messages. Anton was a writer with a perceptive awareness of an audience's expectations and a willingness to conform to such expectations, even if it meant reducing the range of his exploratory methods. It is a worry that Anton, for all that he had internalized my encouragement of his imaginative writing, lacked the confidence to produce it in test contexts. I doubt whether he would have continued to set imaginative writing for himself in his senior-school years as he did during the writing programme. I suspect he would have conformed fairly closely to whatever was expected of him.

John

John remained something of an enigma for me over the period of the study and, partly for this reason, his writing and his attitudes are worth discussing. In neither John's test writing nor his intervention writing can I find evidence of any noticeable development. That is a challenge to explain.

Out of a possible score of 20 for each test letter, John scored 7, 7, 4, 7, and 8 for *Space*, *Peer*, *Kes*, *Principal* and *Future* respectively. With most students in the writing programme I was able to detect aspects of development in their non-test writing, even if they showed little development in their tests. Not so with John. In spite of my best efforts I knew John no better at the end of the study than I did at the beginning. Remarkably, he remained interested in the activities of the writing programme throughout its duration and usually started without demur.

John was the youngest in a family of three sisters and a brother. His father was a mechanic and his mother did home duties. John's ambition was to be a mechanic too. His brother had left school at the earliest opportunity to become a panel beater. John often mentioned the considerable amounts of money he himself could earn in the holidays working for his father. His main interests in life were surfing, bike riding and high jumping at which he was very successful.

When I first met John he said he enjoyed writing and the stories he wrote in class were quite adequate. He had a fairly undifferentiated view of himself as a writer and could not describe himself as either a good, bad, interested or uninterested writer. Over the period of the study his concrete view of himself did not seem to develop towards further abstraction, nor did his view of school or the world around him. His laconic responses in conversation with me or his peers, and his lack of emotional responsiveness attracted my attention. He had learnt that his monosyllabic answers to most questions, if given in a slightly provocative way, could amuse his friends, suggesting that he had learnt how to maintain peer approval, at least.

I sensed ambivalence in John's attitude to me. He had trouble maintaining eye contact and, although he was never hostile, he was hesitant until he was confident I was not going to make life hard for him. He was always punctual to the writing sessions and usually asked what was planned for the day. In his early letters to Edwina, his writing partner, he wrote about his hatred of school and his conflicts with teachers. Maybe the writing sessions were a kind of refuge.

From his written accounts, John apparently antagonized many teachers, and this was understandable. He could create an impression of being simultaneously provocative and naïve. None the less, there was something likeable about John, in spite of his defensively bland manner and lack of contribution to any interactions in the writing sessions. For the most part I think John was closed to school experiences. His defensiveness became more marked over the period of the study. He wrote progressively less in length and the appearance of his handwriting deteriorated to the point of illegibility by the end of Year 9. His self-esteem was enhanced by his sporting achievements and school time was just a long interval between games. Although John always attempted the writing activities in the sessions, he also tried to complete them as quickly as possible. Unfortunately Edwina, his writing partner, was psychologically similar to John with her low self-esteem and there was an element of collusion between them to remain labelled as trouble-makers in school. To me this self-imposed label seemed rather grandiose. Neither John nor Edwina had the energy or leadership qualities to be effective trouble-makers and they were probably nothing more than occasional irritations to teachers. None the less, the label had some purpose in their identity, and in their affinity as writing partners.

There were three significant occasions during the study when John's defensiveness lifted. The first occasion was when he wrote his first free-association piece. He chose, predictably, to report the sights and sound around him in the room. Then he interpolated the comment, 'It is amazing that your mine [sic] can see what is happening.' Later, when I tried to seek further elaboration from John about his reflective comment, he shrugged his shoulders and said nothing.

The second occasion was when John wrote his first letter to Edwina, his writing partner. He wrote the longest, most effective piece of writing he produced over the time of the study. It was forty-four lines long and gave an interesting account of his family and interests. He even showed some awareness of his audience with the rhetorical question, 'Who do you go for in football?' As it happened, Edwina was interested in football but it was indicative of John's egocentricity that he assumed others would share his interests. John was quietly very pleased to receive Edwina's reply to his letter and he wrote, 'This is the first time getting a letter from a girl [sic].' Edwina was also pleased to have a pen-friendship with a boy and there was much to be gained from the fantasy and reality of their relationship. At some level they could see that their writing was providing rewards. Sadly, John and Edwina were not skilled in developing their relationship deeply through their writing. At one point their frustration at not knowing where to go with the friendship was manifest through written abuse to each other – a strategy which indicated their inarticulateness and bewilderment. John, more than Edwina, could not understand nor deal with the abuse, yet Edwina was surprised when his response was to cease writing for a while. For all his well-established defensiveness and lack of affect, John could express his sense of injustice. On one occasion he wrote about teachers who blame the whole class for the misdeeds of one student, and teachers 'who call us names when we can't say anything.' The issue of loss of face in front of peers was a recurring theme in the students' writing and talking.

The third occasion on which John showed an uncharacteristic and this time elaborated (but syntactically inadequate) response to an experience was his written account after hearing my story 'The day Dumbo stopped the class'. The theme of the story was the changed perceptions of a class to one of its members, nicknamed 'Dumbo', after he gave a spoken account of his favourite hobby, making model warships. The class members started to call the boy by his real name and found him interesting. John identified very strongly with the protagonist and wrote: 'the kids shutted up . . . (and) were amazed that he was smart . . . at the end they thought he was a big hero.' The power of literature to help students express unconscious desires and frustrations was apparent in John's writing. It was also a poignant reminder of the well-concealed needs of students like John. In contrast, two months later when John was required to write his response to the *Kes* story, as part of my testing procedures, he wrote, *in toto*, 'Dear Unknown, The story is about a cople of kids smoking and they got busted and went to the principal office and had to empty their pockets and smokes came out and get in trouble [sic] . . .' Not surprisingly, John barely scored at all for this response. We could speculate at length to account for John's lack of response but I think there is a clue in his address to 'Unknown'.

The task of writing with conviction to an unknown audience was beyond his imaginative capacities and real interests. He had also missed the point that he was supposed to be writing to a friend.

John's reluctance to show his feelings was also evident in a letter he wrote to Edwina at the beginning of the third year of the study: 'My Christmas wasn't that great my dog died and he was about 14 years old. My grandma had a car crash and was lucky she wasn't killed and my next door neighbour nearly died over christmas with a heart attack.' As this was written in the March following that Christmas it could be that the matter-of-fact tone of voice reflects the distance in time from these events. But it was also characteristic of John to state events rather than to analyse them or reflect on them. He had adopted the same uninvolved tone when he retold his experience of having twelve stitches in his hand as the result of a surfing accident. He did not seem to recognize the therapeutic effect of expressiveness. The ups and downs of life seemed to affect John with equal indifference. Such an attitude gave rise to some unconscious humour when he wrote to Edwina about his sewing classes: 'I did noting I suposed to make a robe, but I kept playing up and kept putin my hands on my head [the teacher's controlling strategy] and didn't have a chance to start.'

It was noteworthy that the following year, when John wrote his test letter to the principal (*Principal*), arguing the merits of extra-curricular activities, he showed more thought and involvement than might have been expected. Although his point of view was expressed more by dogmatic statements than by reasoned or persuasive logic, there was a sense of a writer trying to grapple with the considerable rhetorical demands of persuasive argument. It could be that John was powerfully influenced by his sense of audience in writing. It could also be that the chance to have his say about school matters was motivating for him. The enabling (and inhibiting) variables in students' motivations for writing often defy easy classification.

In the final year of the study when John was required to write his life-plan letter in the annual test (*Future*), his writing was characterized by slips in tense and syntax – a mark of the instability of his writing development. The content of that letter centred about John's ambition to compete in and win increasingly bigger surfing competitions. His fantasy was to receive life's fortunes by sheer good luck.

His perception of reality was reflected in his conventional fantasies of wish-fulfilment through passivity. ('You can go on the dole all life and still do all the pleasures you would like to do.')

The only significant difference between John's *Space* letter (Year 6) and his *Future* letter (Year 9) was that his *Future* letter was longer, but more egocentric and harder to read than his *Space* letter. At least in the *Space* letter John addressed three rhetorical questions to the spaceman and seemed genuinely interested in his needs. His understanding of writing then was undifferentiated and concrete: 'In school you find reading very hard and writing very easy.' However, at this stage, John's development was not noticeably below average. By the end of Year 9 the length of his *Future* letter only made more obvious his confusion of tenses, his syntactic errors and the inconsistencies in his thought and logic.

John's basic concerns about food, money and pleasure, which emerged through his intervention-programme writing, were strongly present in his *Future* letter. If anything, John showed less awareness of others at the end of Year 9 than he did when he wrote at the end of his *Space* letter, 'Tocarty [his name for the spaceman], I'll teach you how to write it will be fun please come again to our school.' At the end of Year 6 John's class writing showed more mastery of syntactic skills than were evident in his later test writing.

Although John provided me with some insights into his psyche, it was difficult to see any sustained improvement in his thought and language over the time of the study. He liked his relationship with Edwina and was pleased when she invited him to her school dance. He declined the invitation with a degree of social aplomb. However, although he invested some time and effort in his letter writing, he showed little awareness of his own self-absorption and expected that Edwina would enjoy his repeated accounts of his sporting achievements. She was more interested in his accounts of school life and tried to tell him so.

John was not one of life's enthusiasts, yet he seemed well adjusted and contented with his family life and his surfing activities. His declared ambition in life was to make money as a mechanic and to enjoy a comfortable existence. He showed some awareness of the world around him when he expressed in one sentence a wish to stop wars and make peace, but there was no sign of extended interest in the external environment. Even with hindsight it is hard to know what kind of writing programme could have developed John's writing abilities better. Certainly his relationship with Edwina motivated his continued letter writing but, for the most part, those letters were repetitive and self-concerned. It could have been beneficial had he had a more able writer than Edwina as his partner. To develop a better awareness of the demands of written syntax John needed to reread his writing, making the necessary adjustments from spoken language to written language. He rarely bothered to make such changes, often free-associating in inappropriate contexts, assuming, I guess, that the reader would know what he meant.

He was certainly not sufficiently interested enough in his own literacy development to take from his reading or life experiences models for discourse. John is a salutary reminder to curriculum developers and teachers that some students can still defeat the best intentions of our programmes. It is probable that John, like many of his peers, lacked, or was out of touch with, any internal motivation to change because the basic security of his life and the perceived availability of the means to fulfil ambitions reinforced his investment in the status quo. Formal school life did little for him.

It is interesting that the criterion which did account for some increase in John's test-writing scores over the four years was a score of 2 out of 5 for *Creativity* in both his *Principal* letter and his *Future* letter. Tempting as it is, I do not think we can make much of that. His scores on *Language* and *Thinking* showed no increase from *Space* to *Future*.

Once he became involved in a writing task, John could produce a range of details and report several events but his lack of coherence minimized their impact on a reader. I could never persuade John to reread his writing. Once a task was completed, he just sat and stared. Peer pressure was such that I doubt whether he would ever have engaged in peer-group writing activities or conferencing.

Perhaps it is significant that this case study of John is less detailed than others, and its conclusions are more tentative. It is difficult to generalize about John because the consistent trait in his writing and speech was a laconic detachment. Occasional examples countering that (like some of his letters to Edwina) were insufficient to negate the conclusion that John had learned to be purposefully inarticulate or lacked the need or interest to be otherwise.

It is frustrating to admit defeat with a student. John might have gained more out of his letter exchange with Edwina had he had in her a better model for writing. It did happen with some other writing partnerships (like Simon and Juliet) that the more able partner unconsciously modelled for the less able partner methods and strategies for developmental experiences in language, thinking and relating. Of course the able partner needs to be gaining something worthwhile from the experiences too and unequal relationships of this nature rarely last long.

In the case of Edwina and John their expectations of each other could not be met while they were both limited by their egocentricity, and by their inexperience in using language to develop a relationship beyond a superficial stage. Had they been able to disclose more of themselves to each other they might have developed their relationship further, but either they could not make such a move or did not know how to do it anyway. None the less, the uncharacteristic enthusiasm each showed in having a writing partner does suggest that, with further insight into the learning potential of peer relationships, it might be possible to engage students in fruitful writing activities. I am certain that John and Edwina would be early drop-outs from any highly structured writing programme. They needed close, empathic modelling at the point of need and sustained, individual attention.

Implications from the case studies

By their very nature case studies defy easy generalizations. None the less, these stories may have engaged your imagination and you can draw your own conclusions.

I was impressed with the role of psychological processes in the students' intervention writing: processes like the unconscious recognition of the influence of self-esteem in establishing and maintaining a relationship, and the role of self-disclosure in deepening a relationship. Anna and Jane increased my insight into those processes, as did other students in some measure. Some students will disclose their thoughts and feelings to each other, even when they have never met, in a way they would be reluctant to do with a teacher. The power relationships between teachers and students usually preclude mutual self-disclosure.

None the less, the potential for students to reveal and evaluate their feelings, thoughts and experiences through written and spoken dialogues with trusted peers certainly deserves close attention.

The work of the American psychoanalyst Jourard (1971a, 1971b) on the importance of self-disclosure for cognitive and affective development, especially for those who experience life with an intensity of feeling, lends support to my conclusion here that empathic peer relationships can establish an important context for the development of self-knowledge and public knowledge.

In one of Jourard's studies (1971b) he found that when high-disclosing women were paired with high-disclosing women, both subjects were high-disclosing to each other. When high disclosers were paired with low disclosers, the low disclosers became more disclosing. When low disclosers were paired with low disclosers, neither subject became disclosing. You will see parallels with the partnerships I have described. Anna and Jane were both high disclosers and were able to tolerate and work through their conflicts through their disclosures. John and Edwina, both low disclosers, remained so throughout their relationship. One wonders how low disclosers feel when confronted with a positively mute examining audience!

It was interesting that Tanya felt a responsibility to help Lino, her writing partner, by subtly inviting him to reveal more of himself. Regrettably Lino lacked either the strategies, self-awareness or trust to respond effectively to Tanya's efforts. Undoubtedly issues of students' identity, self-worth, reflective capacities, tolerance for frustration and the intensity of their responses to life are significant in all kinds of achievements and developments.

Individuals are infinitely various and complex. Writing-development practices which ignore that piece of common sense will never be effective. If I were to focus on the best insight I gained from my work with the students in the intervention writing programme, I would focus on the richness of the psychological influences upon the students' writing, and on the unpredictable effectiveness of various approaches to writing development. More than ever we need to expand our awareness of what humans can do, in enabling circumstances, and what frustrates their achievements. We need to see each new insight as a small piece in a vast jigsaw puzzle. There is no easy path to human development but attunement to students' feelings and needs and awareness of the mental and psychological functions underlying learning is a prerequisite for effective teaching. I have seen students confront very difficult learning tasks and master them largely because of the presence of an attentive, empathic, significant other. The possibility of an intrinsic reward like a boost in self-esteem is powerfully motivating too. It is a heartening reality for literacy teachers that our students' own talk, writing and life experience are a rich resource for curriculum development. Even the previously negative effects of literacy difficulties can be worked through with sufficient time. But we could never do the task alone. That is why we need to know as much as possible about the tacit and overt abilities, feelings and expectations our students bring with them. Even John had a moment of marvelling at his own mind! Even though we can never teach explicitly the 'universe of discourse' (Moffett 1968), we can motivate students to use language to give expression and shape to felt experience.

It was my own felt experience, partly conveyed here, which motivated the development of the spiral, psychodynamic concept of writing development. I hope you can see now why I think that the self as a unique individual and in relationship with others is the spring to literacy development.

8 What does all this mean in practice?

A theory of writing development underpinned by a student-centred, functional, linguistic and psychological approach necessarily suggests quite complex implications for classroom practice. Teachers implementing this kind of theory need to be able to manage the tension of keeping an open mind about students' capabilities while also being aware of the cognitive, linguistic and psychological determinants and features of writing development. That is asking a lot of even dedicated and hard-working teachers.

One difficulty of this approach is that only so much can be pre-planned. Informed adaptations have to be made as students progress and regress in quite unexpected ways. Hence the need for a comprehensive theory of writing development and sensitive, responsive monitoring of students' writing (and reading and related discourse experiences) over a long period of time. Writing development is slow to occur and difficult to detect by valid measures. To believe otherwise is to ignore the complexity of writing-development processes and possibly to sell our students short.

Let me try to clarify the issues further. Writing teachers (in both senses of the phrase) need to believe that the mind of the writer is both developed and reflected through complex psychological and linguistic processes. That is, authentic composing allows us to develop our minds through the reflexive nature of writing: we can see what we are thinking. That process can generate further thought and increased self-awareness and awareness of others. With that in mind we are in a strong position to make appropriate choices in developing effective writing programmes and to share with our writers the reasons for those choices. Obviously then, collaboration between writers and their teachers is fundamental in negotiating the programme and assessing its effectiveness. Clearly the teacher will need to be able to talk about appropriate features of writing – that is, use the metalanguage of writing development – in order to demystify the process for students. With experience and maturity many students will be able to take over that elaborating and clarifying role – as happens when students collaborate with each other in a conference writing approach.

An effective writing programme needs to be centred upon the communicative intentions of individual writers. We have to be able to determine what those intentions are. That means we have to be sensitive listeners and sensitive readers of their writing. The range of students' intentions can be expanded by the variety of reading and writing they engage in, but pressure to conform to particular forms or genres can never successfully pre-empt the writers' intentions.

Writers do not effectively internalize genres unless they perceive, even unconsciously, that the form of language or genre truly reflects their communicative intentions or purposes. For example, when small children use as an opening phrase for their own stories, 'once upon a time', we know they have a tacit understanding that the phrase establishes a particular format for a series of events and possibilities with infinite implications. The phrase, 'once upon a time' is paradoxical: we all know the stories happen repeatedly, in infinite time, just as we know the phrase signals a narrative structure. Children learn the function of the phrase unconsciously from listening to stories and they can use it effectively because it helps them structure their own narratives. It signals and reflects their expressive and communicative intentions. How could anyone teach that explicitly to a four-year-old? How was a six-year-old able to tell me that she began her story about rock lobsters with the phrase 'If I were a rock lobster I would explore for food'? She had never had lessons in the function of the subjunctive. She had never been told that to express modality and probability there is a particular grammatical structure to use. From her own linguistic experience she had internalized the form and could use it when she needed to. It provided a grammatical structure which matched her particular intentions and, satisfactorily for her, reflected her cognitive and linguistic needs. Again, how could anyone consciously teach the incredibly complex linguistic and cognitive procedures which occur in the process of making meaning? That is why it is essential to connect students with their own potential to make meaning, even if that potential seems limited compared with some norm or standard. If they lose touch with their own potential, they will never generate their own considerable tacit understandings of how language functions.

There is a grave risk that writing practices which truncate the students' deeply internalized wisdom about language will hinder their writing development. We need to know more about that wisdom because it is a fertile source of development. Any premature imposition of adult-classified genres upon the already intricate process of a younger writer's search for, and expression of meaning can only prove alienating and destructive. When students are ready to internalize structures, forms, modes and conventions, they will do so relatively effortlessly, primarily because these match and make explicit their intentions, and expand their expressive repertoire. Hence the need for an enriching range of spoken and written discourses within the environment which can be internalized unconsciously, or consciously when the writer is inclined.

In practical terms that also means that whatever a student writes, or fails to write, is a resource for the development of an individual writing programme for that student. That might sound very daunting but the student and teacher/tutor can work together to determine what the student can/cannot do. The criteria outlines I have given here for *Audience, Creativity, Thinking* and *Language* can provide guidelines for curriculum practices and assessment. They can apply to any number of discourse forms and they are based on a structure which sees writing development evidenced in ability to write for increasingly differentiated audiences and purposes. It is important for students to feel involved in their own writing development. They need to know why certain activities are designed for them. If the criteria for assessing their work, and indeed for responding to it, are made explicit, they are more likely to become effective writers.

Given the vast range of written forms which constitute our world of discourse, it can be overwhelming to have to make choices – for fear that something vital might be overlooked. In reality the world of discourse is manageable if we divide it for convenience's sake, into two broad categories of narrative and argument. I have argued (Arnold 1989) that narrative and argument share more in common than they differ. I do not think we have to be concerned that we 'teach' every kind of discourse if we accept that the universe of discourse is rather better integrated than the classifications of genres would have us believe. If students were to work within the broad division of narrative and argument, experimenting with the important variables of time (present, past, future) and distance (audiences close to or distanced from self), they would have sufficient experiences of writing for most school and life purposes. James Moffett in his seminal book, *Teaching the Universe of Discourse* (1968) contended that growth in discourse is characterized by ability to perceive the world with increased differentiation, and to embed thought in language structures which accurately reflect those differentiated perceptions. Mature writers are able to move across the spectrum of concrete to abstract thought, to record, report, generalize, theorize and speculate, to use language with flexibility and subtlety, to know when to be explicit and when to be implicit. Underpinning those abilities is a cognitive structure which allows them to visualize events in the present, past and future, and audiences close to, or distant from them.

Moffett's writing curriculum handbook, *Student-Centered Language Arts and Reading K-13* (co-authored with B. J. Wagner, 1978), provides an excellent outline for putting his theory into practice. Fortunately it is currently being revised and his *Active Voice* series provides curriculum guidelines and illuminating examples of students' writing. Given the plethora of books full of writing ideas now available, the dilemma is how to cover everything and how to make effective choices. Hence the need for some basic guidelines which take into account the very limited time given in schools to extended writing practice.

If you are concerned that, by following an individualized writing programme with students, you might inadvertently fail to prepare them for public examinations or other standardized assessment procedures, it may help to analyse critically the kinds of language and thinking abilities students need to achieve for such tests. In its variety, integration and implicit/explicit demands a good writing programme should exceed the requirements of formal testing procedures. Apart from writing activities like note-making which are best seen as precursors to extended arguments, free association and expressive writing which can be important for reflective thinking and for developing a self-concept as a writer, telling stories and putting forward points of view can constitute the main kinds of school writing, and they need not be distanced from the students' own concerns. In the public arena, narrative (telling how it has happened, does happen, could happen) and argument (presenting a point of view based on observations/ generalizations or hypothesizing/speculating) are the two most common kinds of writing required. They are also important in their own right for the particular thinking and evaluating abilities they require. Furthermore narrative and argument include features of each other. That is, in narrating events we often put forward points of view, and in arguing we often cite incidents to illustrate our argument. In essence I am arguing that within narratives and arguments there is scope to play the time, audience and purpose variables and to demonstrate speculative/hypothetical thinking. (My earlier example of the six-year-old's construction 'If I were a rock lobster' is an example of rudimentary speculative thinking.)

What I am suggesting is that an individualized writing programme need not, and should not, preclude experiences in those kinds of activities which can both serve the writers' needs and prepare them for assessment tasks. The interplay between public and private demands is one most adults engage in constantly. It is unrealistic not to help students achieve whatever 'glittering prizes' they aspire to, but I think it is best done by focusing primarily on their intrinsic expressive needs and secondarily on the extrinsic needs – in the hope that the interplay between the two will be as smooth as possible. Experiences with both oral and written narratives and arguments can provide a smooth transition between private and public writing.

Where does poetic writing fit in this broad generalization? I believe it can be appropriate in both narrative and argument. Regrettably, poetry writing as such accounts for a very small proportion of school writing (Applebee 1981, Arnold 1987) but I could include it comfortably with both narrative or argument, depending upon whether it records, recounts or evaluates events as in narrative, or presents a point of view as in argument. The rationale here is not just to conflate a vast range of discourse models into two genres, but rather to provide a practical working model for teachers and writing-curriculum developers, bewildered by the complexity of choice. A writing programme which is based on the principles outlined in this book and which provides students with opportunities to write at least narratives and arguments to a variety of audiences and for various purposes (while still engaging the writers' interest) should be effective. Obviously there should be flexibility in any programme for individual choice, provided writers do not become stuck with a limited repertoire.

Conclusion

I have come to the end of my story and the beginning of another one I expect. My work with student writers for four years taught me more than I ever expected and gave me the satisfaction of providing empirical evidence for the value to students' thinking development of certain kinds of imaginative, expressive and authentic writing experiences. Obviously I believe it is possible to give attention to the intrinsic individuality of student writers and promote their growth at the same time. Methods which aim to promote development at the expense of authentic writing, or which ignore the functional pre-eminence of writing experiences for the writers themselves, are likely to prove ineffectual in the long term and thwarting in the short term. There are no short cuts to writing development, and no short cuts to the development of effective writing curricula.

While many researchers, inbued with beliefs of the tacit tradition, espouse case-study design and a deeper understanding of individual writers at work, the discipline of writing development relates to a wide body of scholarship and arguments offered for particular research and teaching methodologies have to be convincing to scholars in both the humanities and the sciences.

Case studies foreground the individual but often lose sense of the generalizable; empirical methods foreground the generalizable while obscuring the individual. I hope I have found a satisfactory balance between the two methods in this book.

I think we need more understanding of effective writing-teaching practices and analyses of the kinds of relationships (between students and their peers as well as teachers and students) in which these practices are put into effect. Clearly I believe the process of developing writing abilities is intrapersonal and interpersonal and there is a need for further insight into the continuity I conjecture in my spiral model between writing for self and for expressive purposes, and writing for more public, informational purposes. While I have demonstrated some continuity between personal and public writing in that the developing experimental writers in my study were demonstrably able to write for increasingly more differentiated audiences and purposes, the nature of that continuity needs further exploration. We need more intensive and long-term studies of good writing teachers at work.

Given the relatively short time available for writing in schools, it would be helpful if descriptive summaries and cumulative records were kept of students' writing development over primary and secondary years, and across all subjects. Students' own perceptions of their development could be part of such records.

The study from which this book arose revealed some of the complexities involved in effecting and assessing a writing programme designed to promote writing development. It raised some questions about the effectiveness of holistic marking methods for determining long-term development, and it provided some evidence of what might be expected in terms of student writing abilities in one mode of writing from Years 6–9 inclusive. It also raised questions about the continuing need for critical philosophical scrutiny of the desirable aims of writing programmes in schools.

In a sense you never leave behind experiences which have involved long-term commitment and my own reflections on student writers still continue. I think that when we put writers in touch with their own capacities to shape thought, feeling and language in written texts, we are helping them to create an individual metaphor for self. If writing can serve that purpose for writers, then it not only demonstrates its intrinsic worth but its potential to create a mature society of integrated individuals in touch with their own cognitive and emotional resources.

In spite of the difficulties of maintaining a long-term research project, when all else fails, it is the sense of empathy and commitment experienced and reciprocated by members of a group sharing some common purpose which makes frustration simply a passing phase in a rite of passage.

If any elaboration or future direction is needed for teachers working in the tacit tradition of Polanyi, Vygotsky, Britton, Moffett and others, I think it could be in developing a more rigorous understanding of the personal relationships conducive to writing development. Hence my interest in developing what I have called a psychodynamic model.

Some of the most intriguing questions about writing development are still unanswered and often unasked. For example, the nature of unconscious processes in writing development, thought and creativity. Simon's comment about 'the magic in the brain' is a salutory reminder of students' power to create insight and meaning from certain writing experiences.

Expressive and authentic writing can tell us much about the symbolizing and integrating power of the human psyche. It is idiosyncratic to writing that we can create written discourse and simultaneously reflect on that creation by reading our writing. It may be that writing processes which are experienced as self-enhancing and self-discovering because they allow us to create meaning and reflect upon it stimulate levels of abstract thought and the co-operation of unconscious powers. The notion needs investigation.

When transactional language is unequal to the task, of necessity we resort to metaphor, if possible. The experience of engaging with student writers over a long time, and the sense of awe I felt in observing their personal, often difficult search for meaning in written language gave me some insights into the integrating power of authentic language.

In essence this psychodynamic theory of writing development is a response to witnessing and experiencing writing as a deeply felt human need to

bind in a spell
the tale of our own creation.

Appendix A
The writing intervention research project

This appendix gives details of the four-year study during which I tested the effects of an intervention writing programme on a group of students.

The research design

In summary, I worked as a researcher/teacher with two groups of students in two metropolitan Sydney schools for a period of four years, from school years 6 to 9 inclusive. That included the last year of primary school and the first three years of secondary school. There were thirty-five students in the total group, split fairly evenly between the two schools. One school was an all girls' private school (school A), the other a co-ed government-funded school (school B). Within the group there was a representative sample of students with a working-class, mainly migrant background and students from the professional middle class.

The major hypothesis of the study

The major hypothesis of the study was that a writing intervention programme which was designed to stimulate writers to focus and edit their inner speech and to reflect on their own thoughts and feelings in writing would improve their ability to write. Ability to write was defined as an increased ability to differentiate audience, purpose, thought, feeling and language. In essence, the hypothesis was designed to determine whether basic expressiveness was a core motivation for writing development.

A brief outline of the study

The study involved my working with the experimental students for one lesson a fortnight on a writing intervention programme. To gather data on the writing abilities of both the experimental students and their peers, I set a particular test writing task each year which was undertaken by the students in six schools, in the grade parallel to that of the experimental students. There are details of those test topics and a discussion of related issues in chapter 3 where assessment procedures and the development of the four criteria for writing development are also outlined.

Nature of the intervention programme

In accordance with the hypothesis being tested in the study, and with the beliefs informing it, the writing experiences undertaken by the experimental students initially involved expressive writing directed to the self as audience. Over time the writers began to write to audiences other than self, as will be seen in the report below of the letter-writing exchange, and they began to write with increased differentiation. Briefly, increased differentiation in thought and language means the writer is able to report on experiences or create imagined experiences and reflect on them in increasingly more complex ways. A simple example of differentiation is the process by which small children might initially classify all flying objects as birds, then gradually realize that flying objects may also be butterflies, kites or scraps of paper. Of course, as with any group of individual learners, there were variations in the patterns of writing, amounts of writing completed and approaches to writing chosen by the students. None the less, the main feature of the programme was the encouragement given to the students to find their own writing voice and to develop an awareness of their own thoughts, feelings and responses through an interplay between reflections on experiences and writing. Some models of writing were provided by the letters subsequently exchanged between writing partners in the experimental groups, and on occasions in the later years of the study I read stories to the groups as a stimulus to writing. For the most part, the intervention programme involved the students finding the content for their writing from their own experiences and from their responses to their letter-writing partners. Clearly an effective writing programme needs to involve students in experiences with a wide range of discourse models. A full-time classroom writing curriculum would need to extend the range of experiences I offered the students by providing such models at appropriate times. For various practical reasons, my time with the students was limited to one session a fortnight, and even these were often frustrated by the various interruptions to school routines with which we are all familiar.

An overview of the intervention writing programme

After some preliminary sessions with the students in the experimental groups to establish the purposes of the programme and to develop a positive working relationship with them, I asked them to undertake some meditative, focused concentration exercises, similar to those often undertaken in drama or relaxation classes. Briefly, the students were asked to select a place in the room to which they would return to do their writing, to set up their writing materials ready for work, then to lie on the floor with eyes closed, focusing on the thoughts and feelings they were aware of. My role was to talk the students into a relaxed frame of mind by calmly and quietly giving the instructions and by establishing a peaceful environment. My work as a drama teacher had given me experience in this kind of exercise. I felt comfortable, and confident of its value, a prerequisite for a teacher working in this way.

After about two to three minutes of relaxation, the students were asked to return to their working space and to record their responses. Without fail, all students did some writing and the atmosphere in the room was one of high productivity and self-involvement. Several students spontaneously commented on the unexpected pleasure of the experience and asked to repeat it. As well as reporting what they had witnessed in their own minds, some made comments such as: 'That is the first time I have known what I think,' or 'I could go on doing this for ever.'

After three sessions of free-association writing, I tried to encourage more sustained reflective writing, particularly that which involved projecting into the future and examining past experiences. I was mindful here of the need to vary the time span for students' writing, just as we need to vary the cognitive dimensions by having students write for audiences close to and distant from self. We can be guided in our choice of appropriate occasions to set differing expectations for students' writing only by our understanding of their capacities and by our flexibility in handling the students' success or failure. It goes almost without saying that students must feel comfortable about experimenting with their writing and valued for their attempts as much as for their achievements. It is difficult to hold on to this value in a school or community embued with a materialistic, competitive ethos, but, as the empirical results of this study show, interactionist, psychodynamic approaches to writing can positively influence students' thinking, at least.

Subsequent writing sessions started with the writers' focused concentration on a recalled learning experience. They were asked to recall and reflect upon a significant learning experience such as learning to ride a bike or a skateboard, or learning to read or to develop some skill. In the pre-writing discussion I asked the students to think about the person who might have helped them to learn the new skill, to reflect on their feelings and memories of that event. I also asked them to draw conclusions, if possible, about how one learns best. In effect I was encouraging them to move from personal experience to generalization. As might be expected, that part of the task proved too difficult for some of the writers. None the less, I think it is important to provide extension work for those who can take up the invitation. For the next reflective piece I suggested that writers imagine they were writing to a primary-school student. The task was to describe and reflect upon a world in which everything would be edible. While the students had to imagine such a situation, they could also envisage quite readily an audience younger than themselves. In effect they could write as 'experts'.

In the pre-writing discussion, writers shared their fantasies and ideas with other group members. What was interesting about that exercise was not only the imaginative stories which were written, but the spontaneous discussion about story-telling techniques which arose after the writing. Some students articulated an awareness of the processes of writing, demonstrating the rudiments of a metalanguage to discuss these processes. From then on, most writing sessions started with an informal but guided discussion about issues relevant to the writing task to be undertaken. I believe that, when students feel centred in their writing, they do become more conscious of and more curious about underlying techniques. They also begin to notice how other writers craft their work.

After about ten sessions of free association and then of guided and focused work, students were conscious of the potential wealth of writing content within their own memories and feelings. The degree of consciousness, and of self-confidence varied, of course, but in both groups there was a sense of purpose and of group cohesiveness.

The letter-writing exchange

The next major shift in focus in the intervention programme was the start of the letter-writing exchange. The students were now in Year 7, their first year in secondary school. By the middle of that year they were well settled into the writing programme and it was well established. I was considering ways of extending the students' writing from the personal, writing-mainly-for-self pieces which they had been doing to date, to writing tasks directed to close others. I sensed they were ready for some developmental shift and was considering what form that should take, when one of the girls in the group asked if they could write letters to the students in the other experimental school. Both groups of students had become interested in our writing research and they were curious about their peers in the other group. There was a strong sense of identification with the project and with each other.

The response to the idea of the letter-writing exchange was so spontaneous and enthusiastic that it could not be ignored. It was also consistent with the principles underlying my own teaching and research that a student-initiated idea could be powerful and important. I took the idea seriously, even though it meant rethinking the research design. The two groups would now be interacting with and influencing each other. None the less, the idea had all the power of a real discovery and, in retrospect, my hesitation seemed faint-hearted. At that stage I could not see how to account for the possible influence of the exchange on the students' writing development. That problem solved itself once I analysed the letters. Apart from the students' enthusiasm for the idea, it felt as if to reject it without a plausible explanation would have been a betrayal of my basic trust in the students' abilities to direct their own learning. The idea was put into action.

Arbitrarily I gave each writer in the group at school A the name of a student in the group at school B. The only variation to reading down a random list of names was when two girls in school A asked to write to a boy in school B (there was an imbalance in the male-female ratio).

The research notes taken after the first letter-writing session record a sense of excitement in group A when they started writing their first letter to a partner in the other school. The opportunity to make contact with another writer in the research project led to all kinds of fantasies about shared weekends away and further contact. There was also some challenge to the writers in making public now their to-date private and exploratory writing.

On reflection, it was timely that the letter-writing idea arose when it did. With emerging adolescence the students were becoming more peer-oriented. Until this, the students in the intervention programme had been involved in concentrated, private, self-revealing writing which for some had created a demonstrable change in their self-perception as a writer. Sarah, a member of a remedial English class in Year 6 had had a very low opinion of her language abilities. In the first letter-writing session she said:

> Last year I didn't do well in English. I used to go home and say 'What will I write about, Mum?' I could never think how to do a story. This year I got good marks in English. Mum and I think it's because of this (research project). I know how to write now. I can do it. It's much better.

Whether Sarah's change in marks and in self-perception is wholly attributable to the writing sessions or not is difficult to know but at least it is clear that she felt better about herself as a writer now, and she was ready to reach out to a more public audience. Self-confidence and perceived relevance can make a significant difference.

The letter-writing exchange started a sequence of writing activities which continued for the next two-and-a-half years. It provided evidence of the writers' intuitive abilities in establishing and maintaining a relationship through their own writing, as well as offering insights into writing processes which were not anticipated when the exchange started. For example, the energy, interest and commitment the writers sustained in continuing the exchange, even after an eight-week break over the Christmas vacation, raised questions about the psychological importance of writing for students' self-development, and about the power of peer relationships in school learning.

From the beginning of the letter exchange to the end of the first year of its operation (the second year of the research project), seven letters were exchanged between the two groups with my acting as courier. The writers understood that I would read the letters at some time. This did not seem to cause any obvious problems. There were times when the writers asked for assurance that no one other than I and their writing partner would read their letters. At first the letters were written on sheets of regular school-work writing pads; then I provided writing booklets which helped to keep the letters in their correct sequence. The writing partners shared the booklets, writing their letters in turn. I filed the booklets in a folder in the partners' names. From time to time I would bring the whole folder to the sessions for the writers to read back over their earlier letters. Some found this review process very interesting. Occasionally they were embarrassed to recall how much effort they had expended on writing about some issue which had long since been resolved. Sometimes letters or parts of them would be shared with other members of the writing group. There was a strong sense of ownership of letters from a writing partner, and a sense of bonding between the partners, so the need for privacy often pre-empted sharing.

The letter-writing exchange continued for the third and fourth year of the research project. As well, the writers who had finished their letters quickly often wrote further reflective pieces, or spontaneous monologues or composed observation pieces. There were some writers in each group who needed further acceleration and were willing to continue writing after the regular class time. For the composed observation pieces, the writers sat quietly in the classroom or outside, jotting down notes of details they observed around them for later use in writing a sustained piece of descriptive or reflective writing. Sometimes this exercise stimulated a train of thought which became the content of a letter. The principle guiding the method was that of building up material for writing by abstracting from details. For some writers, the concrete experience of noting details from the immediate environment gave form to their writing when memory alone was insufficient. I would then discuss with the writers how they could make personal notes and collect information from books and other sources in order to write up information and experiences in other school subjects.

I was consciously trying to help the writers to feel that the acquisition of knowledge could be a personal experience, symbolized and made meaningful through their own writing and talking. In the context of the kinds of writing they had been doing in the writing programme, the point made sense to them. However, I discovered from the data collected later on the kinds of writing down across the curriculum in the two research schools that my approach was rarely reinforced in the regular classrooms.

Sometimes I would read short stories to the writers, as a source of ideas or to provide for the exchange of opinions in their letters. On one occasion I read them one of my stories published in a newspaper. The theme of the story was the recognition by a teacher of the hidden talents of one of her students, and the changed perceptions of his classmates when his abilities were revealed. The writers identified readily with the character in the story and discussed the story at length. Some writers wrote about their responses in their letters to their partners.

Towards the end of the third year of the programme, the writers were more able to set their own writing tasks as they had a range of options to choose from, either within the letter format or separate from that. The more able writers wrote extended fantasies, stories and reminiscences, as well as their letters. Some of these pieces formed part of a Christmas journal which each writing group in the two schools exchanged with each other.

By the fourth year of the writing intervention programme there was a noticeable difference between some of the boys in school B and their writing partners in the all-girls school A. The girls, with a couple of exceptions, were bored with the often repetitive content of the boys' letters. Although I suggested that the girls could prompt their writing partners about ways they might make their letters more interesting, the goodwill of the girls was soon eroded when some of the boys failed to change the theme of their letters (usually sport) or resorted to an undifferentiated accumulation of detail. On a couple of occasions one boy writer made up a fantasy about his fabulous sporting achievements to win the girl's admiration. Weary of this theme, his writing partner, Susan, made up her own fantasy about her achievements as a famous ballet dancer. Even here her attempt was noticeably more sophisticated and interesting than her partner's, with an ironic undercurrent adding humour to her work. While continuing the letter-writing exchange, some girls also started to write their own fantasies and stories where the audience was non-specific, though I was usually invited to read the pieces. By now the writers could set their own pace and content for writing, though sometimes I would prompt them, if necessary, with opening statements like 'I feel annoyed when . . .', 'If I could change something in the world I would' . . ., or 'I wish I could . . .'.

Sometimes I read to the groups poems by young writers in published anthologies in the hope that they might write poetry themselves. The few poems they did write tended to be trite and mechanistic. Rarely were the poems reworked or even deeply felt. Regrettably, there was a general resistance to poetry writing, except from a couple of writers who felt they had some poetry-writing technique. The most effective poetic writing emerged unconsciously in prose or narrative pieces.

One method which worked well when I was trying to extend the thinking and range of points of view in the writers was a series of letters written in response to a fictitious advertisement inviting young people to stay in a country home here or abroad. The writers had to write a reply to the advertisement, a return letter from the advertiser, and another reply from themselves as the applicant acknowledging the advertiser's letter and confirming travel arrangements. Finally, they had to write a letter of thanks after their return home from the imagined visit. The changes in point of view which these letters required called for considerable imaginative ability, the selection of appropriate information, style, tone of voice, and a degree of self-presentation. It was a worthwhile exercise and could be elaborated upon with further extension work. For example, one boy writer spontaneously wrote an imaginary journal about his stay in the country.

Some comments on the writing intervention programme

While the above outline gives some idea of the kinds of activities undertaken in the intervention programme throughout the years, it is difficult to describe adequately the atmosphere and on-going relationships within the programme. It is an obvious shortcoming of this kind of research, where the researcher-teacher has to play a dual role, that some emphases take precedent over others and the range of observations are limited and subjective. As in any classroom, it was difficult to give close attention to one particular student and to take note of all the attitudes, behaviours and changes occurring within the group.

I took notes as frequently as possible of incidents and comments of relevance to understanding writing processes, but a different kind of study could look more closely at the role of the writing teacher in a long-term relationship with students. It was certainly helpful to me when the students began to write about their own writing processes, reflecting on their experiences and self-perceptions, and demonstrating a metacognitive awareness of the process.

The most difficult but gratifying part of the intervention programme to describe is the relationship I had with the students. We always liked seeing each other and developed strong bonds over the time of the study. In some cases we have kept in touch over the years. Given the high retention rate of students (only three dropped out by choice at the end of the first year because they wanted to do more work in mathematics rather than in writing), it seems the programme held their interest. The level of motivation in the sessions was consistently in a range of moderate to very high. The interest expressed by most of the students in attending the sessions and in discovering that writing could be an enjoyable and self-revealing experience, suggests that these writers perceived accurately my belief in their capacities as writers and in their need to find their own writing voice.

Since the study finished I have analysed further my role in the writing intervention programme, especially in terms of the relationships I had with the students. I now believe that what happened in the programme was a process of transference, as the psychoanalysts call it. That is, the students believed that, as a writing teacher-researcher, I valued writing. They knew I loved books and writing and they believed that I could pass something of value on to them. There is nothing specially remarkable about that – that part of the transference process operates in most effective teaching contexts. What is important to note though is that I believed in turning around the students' idealization of my abilities so that they could activate their own writing abilities. The main function of good teaching is not to have students fixated in admiration for the teacher, important as that may be to start the process, but for the teacher to mirror back to the students respect for their meaning-making abilities. The process can be reciprocal, of course, but good writing teachers will give primary focus to the students' abilities, using their own empathic understanding of what is involved in writing and learning to guide their responses to the students. It may seem self-evident to talk about the teacher's role in this way, but I think we take for granted much that is important about good teaching. It helps to differentiate more finely what does go on between students and teachers, often unconsciously, in enabling contexts. Psychoanalysis, which has much to offer educators in understanding the nature of relationships and their often hidden agenda, can provide useful insights into some of the unconscious and powerful aspects of the process.

Self-psychologists like Kohut (1971, 1977, 1978, 1985) have built an impressive theory of self-development around the transference phenomenon, the influence of mirroring experiences, the empathic quality between parents and children and the positive influence of others whom we might regard as 'a twin'. For years good teachers have been the exemplifying aspects of those processes. If we consider even briefly the nature of the relationship between a parent/attentive adult and a small child learning to speak, we can witness the skilful mirroring of admiration the adult offers the child in warmly acknowledging his/her attempts at utterance. The adult responds as if those utterances make sense and prompts the child to differentiate the utterance by repeating what he/she thinks the child is trying to say. All in a context of mutual positive regard. While acknowledging with respect Halliday's (1975) theory that children learn language because they know what language does, I suspect that in future we will need to pay more attention to the nature and quality of the relationships between children learning to develop their language abilities and their teachers/mentors/peers. As you can see in the case studies earlier, the nature of the relationship between writing partners like Anna and Jane influenced both the content of their writing, their desire to match their partners and their ability to identify and resolve conflicts between them.

Summary

- The intervention writing programme involved various writing tasks which encourage writers to be reflective and self-revealing in searching for their own writing voice.
- When the writers had gained sufficient experience in writing for their own purposes, they sought other audiences for their writing, as with the letter-writing exchange between the writers in the two experimental schools. These letters revealed the students' ability to establish and maintain effective relationships through their own writing and to develop a sense of writing for a significant reader.
- An enabling relationship between a writing teacher and his/her students needs close analysis in terms of its dynamics. Teachers need to be aware of their deepest attitudes and beliefs about language development, teaching and learning, because these aspects exert a powerful influence, even unconsciously.

Appendix B
Janes's test writing

(i) Jane's test writing: Space – Year 6

Dear Mr Bajeucatastrophsappliangupleeeee V

I'm writing to tell you a little bit about our Creative Writing. I suppose you think it rather strange? Well, personally so do I sometimes but most of the time I find it quite enjoyable. We have someone who comes in twice a term to talk about our writing, so I often do writing at home to show her. *(somehow I have the feeling you know her). What I like best is poems on moving things or feelings, and stories with a bit of comedy in them. I find them hard when just told to write on 1 boring subject it is much easier when you are given the choice of quite a few interesting topics to take a pick from.

We do it so as to use our imagination I suppose. Sometimes we read them to the class. I think that's for our speech and acknowledgement of punctuation. We do Creative Writing about once a week sometimes more.

I hope you understand more about creative writing because of this letter.

Your Good Friend,

X

(ii) Jane's test writing: Future – Year 9

Dear Faith,

As I have probably told you tomorrow is the big day. I am going to the 'life-plan' agent to consult him about my life. For the past weeks I have been wracking by brains to think of the 'ideal' life! It really is so hard!! There are so many different events to choose from and then I have to put them together in some kind of chronological order. It is difficult but enjoyable. As you know the old saying 'anticipation is half the pleasure'. Just looking at all the wonderful ideas is mind boggling. It really amazing how life has progressed in the last century! When we do history at school we learn all about how the 'proto-people' of the 1980's had to just live life and wait for things to happen! They had no say in the matter. How boring!!! Well anyway, after a lot of sorting, choosing, changing my mind and choosing again I have finally decided. I'm really excited about it and can't wait to start. Of course the first things that come to mind are power, wealth and glory but when you think about it there are really so many sub-topics. By the way have you heard that they are going to lower the age limit of pick your life plan' from ten to seven. I hope so for the sake of the children of the future! Mind you, I suppose at the age of seven you are not quite ready to decide your life!

Anyway now that I'm 10 my time has finally come up. Yours will too soon!!

I have decided that as I grow up I will join the 'Worldwide Theatre Co.' For a few years. I am going to be an actress of the best kind. I will travel the world and find something new and exciting each time. When I am twenty-four I am going to meet a man from Switzerland who is very rich. The money is not important, it is the things we will see, places we will go and people we will meet together that I care about. I will of course graciously retire from the world of theatre to marry this man. We will be married in 'The Vatican Cathedral' in style and glory.

After a few years of glorious living I am going to travel to the desolate countries and set up huge 'help' centres. I will not mind spending my money this way, in fact I will enjoy it as I will have spent so much on myself already. I will go to each country and help the people and leaders of each country.

[Writer wrote 'not finished' here.]

References and bibliography

Andrews, R. (ed.) (1989). *Narrative and Argument*. Milton Keynes, Open University Press.

Applebee, A. N. (1981). *Writing in the Secondary School*. Urbana, Ill., National Council of Teachers of English, National Council of Teachers of English Report no. 21.

——(1986). 'Problems in process approaches; towards a reconceptualization of process instruction', in Petrosky, A. and Bartholomae, D. (eds.) *The Teaching of Writing*, Eighty-fifth Yearbook of the National Society for the Study of Education, Part 11. Chicago, Ill., distributed by the University of Chicago Press.

Arnold, R. (ed.) (1983a). *Timely Voices*. Melbourne, Oxford University Press.

——(1983b). 'How to make the audience clap: children's writing and self-esteem', in Arnold, R. (ed.). *Timely Voices*. Melbourne, Oxford University Press.

——(1987). 'A longitudinal study of school children's writing abilities (school) years 6–9 inclusive', unpublished Ph.D thesis, University of Sydney.

——(1989). 'A telling argument from children's arguments and narratives' in Andrews, R. (ed.). *Narrative and Argument*. Milton Keynes, Open University Press.

Atwell, N. (1987). *In the Middle: Writing, Reading, and Learning with Adolescents*. Portsmouth, NH, Boynton Cook/Heinemann.

Bennett, B., Bowes, D., Jeffery, C., McPhail, S., Sooby, A. and Walker, A. (1980). 'An investigation of the process of writing and the development of writing abilities 15–17', Canberra: Report to the Education Research and Development Committee.

Bereiter, C. and Scardamalia, M. (1982). 'From conversation to composition: the role of instruction in a developmental process', in Glaser, R. (ed.). *Advances in Instructional Psychology*, vol. 2. Hillsdale, NJ, Lawrence Erlbaum Associates.

Britton, J. N., Martin, N. C. and Rosen, H. (1966). 'Multiple marking of English compositions: an account of an experiment.' *Schools Council Examinations Bulletin*, no. 12. London, HMSO.

Britton, J. N., Burgess, T., Martin, N., McLeod, A. and Rosen, H. (1975). *The Development of Writing Abilities (11–18)*, London, Macmillan Education.

Bruner, J. S. (1972). *The Relevance of Education*. Harmondsworth, Penguin.

——(1986). *Actual Minds, Possible Worlds*. Cambridge, MA, and London, Harvard University Press.

Calkins, L. (1985). *The Art of Teaching Writing*. Portsmouth, NH, Heinemann.

Cardinal, M. (1984). *The Words to Say It*. London, Picador/Pan.

Cooper, C. R. and Odell, L. (eds.) (1977a). *Evaluating Writing: Describing, Measuring, Judging*. Urbana, Ill., National Council of Teachers of English.

Cooper, C. R. (1977b). 'Holistic evaluation of writing' in Cooper, C. R. and Odell, L. (eds.). *Evaluating Writing: Describing, Measuring, Judging*. Urbana, Ill., National Council of Teachers of English.

Covington, M. V. and Beery, R. G. (1976). *Self-Worth and School Learning*. New York, Holt, Rinehart & Winston.

Cowie, H. (ed.) (1984). *The Development of Children's Imaginative Writing*. London and Canberra, Croom Helm.

Cox Report (1989). *English for Ages 5 to 16*. London, Department of Education and Science/HMSO.

Dixon, J. (1975). *Growth Through English*. London, Oxford University Press.

Donaldson, M. (1978). *Children's Minds*. London, Fontana Collins.

Emig, J. (1971). *The Composing Processes of Twelfth Graders*. Urbana, Ill., National Council of Teachers of English.

——(1980). 'The tacit tradition: the inevitability of a multi-disciplinary approach to writing research' in Freedman, A. and Pringle, I. (eds.). *Reinventing the Rhetorical Tradition*. Conway, AR, L&S Books and Canadian Council of Teachers of English.

——(1981). 'Non-magical thinking: presenting writing developmentally in schools' in Frederiksen, C. and Dominic, J. (eds.). *Writing: The Nature, Development, and Teaching of Written Communication*, vol. 2. Hillsdale, NJ, Lawrence Erlbaum Associates.

——(1983). *The Web of Meaning: Essays on Writing, Teaching, Learning and Thinking*. Goswami, D. and Butler, M. (eds.). Upper Montclair, NJ, Boynton Cook.

Freud, S. (1938). 'Mistakes in reading and writing' in *The Basic Writings of Sigmund Freud*. Brill, A. A. (ed.). New York, Random House.

Goffman, E. (1969). *The Presentation of Self in Everyday Life*. London, Allen Lane.

Graves, D. H. (1979). 'Patterns of growth in the writing processes of young children', paper presented at the Canadian Council for Teachers of English Conference, Ottawa.

——(1981). 'Writing research for the eighties: what is needed'. *Language Arts*, 58, 2.

——(1982). 'Patterns of child control of the writing process' in Eagleson, R. D. (ed.). *English in the Eighties*. Adelaide, Australian Association for the Teaching of English.

——(1983). *Teachers and Children at Work*. Exeter, NH, Heinemann Educational Books.

Halliday, M. A. K. (1969). 'Relevant models of language'. *Educational Review*, 22, 1, 26–37.

——(1973). *Explorations in the Functions of Language*. London, Edward Arnold.

——(1975). *Learning How to Mean: Explorations in the Development of Language*. London, Edward Arnold.

——(1978). *Language as Social Semiotic: The Special Interpretation of Language and Meaning*. London, Edward Arnold.

Harris, J. and Wilkinson, J. (eds.) (1986). *Reading Children's Writing: A Linguistic View*. London, Allen & Unwin.

Harrison, B. T. (1983). *Learning Through Writing: Stages of Growth in English*. Windsor, National Foundation for Educational Research/Nelson Publishing.

Hillocks, G. (1986). 'The writer's knowledge: theory, research and implications for practice' in Petrosky, A. and Bartholomae, D. (eds.). *The Teaching of Writing*, Eighty-fifth Yearbook of the National Society for the Study of Education, Part 11, Chicago, Ill., distributed by the University of Chicago Press.

Hines, B. (1979). *Kes – A Kestrel for a Knave*. Harmondsworth, Penguin.

Johnston, B. (1982). 'Motivational effects of different schemes for assessing students' writing' in Eagleson, R. D. (ed.). *English in the Eighties*. Adelaide, Australian Association for the Teaching of English.

——(1987). *Assessing English*. Milton Keynes, Open University Press.

Jourard, S. M. (1971a). *The Transparent Self* (rev. edn). New York, Van Nostrand Reinhold.

——(1971b). *Self Disclosure: An Experimental Analysis of the Transparent Self*. New York, Wiley-Interscience.

Kelly, G. (1955). *The Psychology of Personal Constructs*. New York, W. W. Norton.

——(1963). *The Theory of Personality*. New York, W. W. Norton.

Kinneavy, J. L. (1971). *A Theory of Discourse*. Englewood Cliffs, NJ, Prentice Hall.

——(1980). 'A pluralistic synthesis of four contemporary models for teaching composition' in Freedman, A. and Pringle, I. (eds.). *Reinventing the Rhetorical Tradition*. Conway, AR, L&S Books and Canadian Council of Teachers of English.

Kohut, H. (1971). *The Analysis of the Self*. New York, International Universities Press.

——(1977). *The Restoration of the Self*. New York, International Universities Press.

——(1978). *The Search for the Self: Selected Writings of Heinz Kohut 1950–1978*. Ornstein, P. (ed.). New York, International Universities Press.

——(1984). *How Does Analysis Cure?* Goldberg, A. (ed.) with Stepansky, P. Chicago, University of Chicago Press.

——(1985). *Self Psychology and the Humanities*. New York, W. W. Norton.

Luria, A. R. (1969). 'Speech development and the formation of mental processes' in Cole, M. and Maltzman, I. (eds.). *A Handbook of Contemporary Soviet Psychology*. New York, Basic Books.

——(1973). *The Working Brain: An Introduction to Neuro-Psychology*. New York, Basic Books.

——(1976). *Cognitive Development: Its Cultural and Social Foundations*. Cambridge, MA, Harvard University Press.

Martin, N. (1983). *Mostly About Writing: Selected Essays by Nancy Martin*. Upper Montclair, NJ, Boynton Cook.

Mayher, J. S., Lester, N. B. and Pradl, G. M. (1983). *Learning to Write/Writing to Learn*. Upper Montclair, NJ, Boynton Cook.

Mead, G. H. (1964). 'Self' in Strauss, A. (ed.). *On Social Psychology: Selected Papers*. Chicago, University of Chicago Press.

Meek, M. (1983). *Achieving Literary*. London, Routledge & Kegan Paul.

Moffett, J. (1968). *Teaching the Universe of Discourse*. Boston, Houghton Mifflin.

——(1981a). *Coming on Center – English Education in Evolution*. Montclair, NJ, Boynton Cook.

——(1981b). *Active Voice – A Writing Program across the Curriculum*. Montclair, NJ, Boynton Cook.

——(1985). 'Liberating inner speech'. *College Composition and Communication*, 36, 3, 304–8.

Moffett, J. and Tashlik, P. (1987). *Active Voices 11 – A Writer's Reader for Grades 7–9*. Upper Montclair, NJ, Boynton Cook.

Moffett, J. and Wagner, B. J. (1976). *Student-Centered Language Arts and Reading K-13 – A Handbook for Teachers* (2nd edn). Boston, Houghton Mifflin.

Moffet, J., Wixon, P., Wixon, V., Blau, S. and Phreaner, J. (1987). *Active Voices 111 – A Writer's Reader for Grades 10–12*. Upper Montclair, NJ, Boynton Cook.

Murray, D. M. (1978). 'Internal revision: a process of discovery' in Cooper, C. and Odell, L. (eds.). *Research on Composing: Points of Departure*. Urbana, Ill., National Council of Teachers of English.

Myers, M. (1980). *A Procedure for Writing Assessment and Holistic Scoring*. Urbana, Ill., National Council of Teachers of English and Educational Resources Information Centre.

——(1985). *The Teacher-Researcher: How to Study Writing in the Classroom*. Urbana, Ill., National Council of Teachers of English and ERIC.

Newkirk, T. (1985). 'The hedgehog or the fox: the dilemma of writing development'. *Language Arts*, 62, 6, 593–603.

——(1986). *To Compose: Teaching Writing in the High School*. Portsmouth, NH, Heinemann Educational.

O'Donnell, H. (1984). 'The effect of topic on writing performance'. ERIC/Clearinghouse on Reading and Communication Skills Report, *English Education*, 16, 4, 243–9.

Piaget, J. (1955). *The Child's Construction of Reality* (trans. M. Cook). London, Routledge & Kegan Paul.

——(1959). *Language and Thought of the Child* (trans. H. Weaver). London: Routledge & Kegan Paul.

——(1978). *Success and Understanding*. London, Routledge & Kegan Paul.

Piaget, J. and Inhelder, B. (1958). *The Growth of Logical Thinking from Childhood to Adolescence*. New York, Basic Books.

——(1969). *The Psychology of the Child* (trans. H. Weaver). London, Routledge & Kegan Paul.

Pickering, D. (1986). 'Writing as thinking in a successful basic skills program'. *Journal of Educational Opportunity*, 1, 1.

Polanyi, M. (1959). *The Study of Man*. Chicago, University of Chicago Press.

——(1962). *Personal Knowledge: Towards a Post-critical Philosophy*. London, Routledge & Kegan Paul.

——(1967). *The Tacit Dimension*. New York, Anchor Books.

——(1969). *Knowing and Being – Essays by Michael Polanyi*. M. Grene (ed.). Chicago, University of Chicago Press.

Pradl, G. M. (ed.) (1982). *Prospect and Retrospect – Selected Essays of James Britton*. Montclair NJ, Boynton Cook/Heinemann Educational.

Pringle, I. and Freedman, A. (1984). 'A comparative study of writing abilities in two modes at the Grade 5, 8 and 12 levels: a report for the Ministry of Education, Ontario.' Department of Linguistics, Carleton University.

Rentel, V. and King, M. (1983). 'Present at the beginning' in Mosenthal, P., Tamor, L. and Walmsley, S. A. (eds.). *Research in Writing: Principles and Methods*. New York and London, Longman.

Rogers, C. (1969). *Freedom to Learn: A View of What Education Might Become*. Columbus, OH, Merrill.

——(1977). *Carl Rogers on Personal Power*. New York, Delacorte Press.

——(1983). *Freedom to Learn for the 80s*. Columbus, OH, Merrill.

Scardamalia, M. (1981). 'How children cope with the cognitive demands of writing' in Frederikson, C. H., Dominic, C. H. and J. H. (eds.). *Writing: The Nature, Development and Teaching of Written Composition*, vol. 2. Hillsdale, NJ, Lawrence Erlbaum Associates.

Smith, F. (1982). *Writing and the Writer*. London, Heinemann Educational.

——(1983). 'Reading like a writer'. *Language Arts*, 60, 5.

Styles, M. (ed.) (1989). *Collaboration and Writing*. Milton Keynes, Open University Press.

Voss, R. F. (1983). 'Janet Emig's *The Composing Processes of Twelfth Graders*: a re-assessment'. *College Composition and Communication*, 34, 278–83.

Vygotsky, L. S. (1962). *Thought and Language*. Cambridge, MA, MIT Press.

——(1978). 'The prehistory of written language' in Cole, M., John-Steiner, V., Scribner, S. and Souberman, E. (eds.). *Mind in Society: The Development of Higher Psychological Processes*. Cambridge, MA, Harvard University Press.

White, M. T. and Weiner, M. B. (1986). *The Theory and Practice of Self Psychology*. New York, Brunner/Mazel.

Wilkinson, A. (1986a). *The Quality of Writing*. Milton Keynes, Open University Press.

Wilkinson, A. (ed.) (1986b). *The Writing of Writing*. Milton Keynes, Open University Press.

Wilkinson, A., Barnsley, G., Hanna, P. and Swan, M. (1980). *Assessing Language Development*. Oxford, Oxford University Press.

Young, J. Z. (1978). *Programs of the Brain*. Oxford, Oxford University Press.

Index